Reteaching
and Practice
Workbook

Kindergarten

Scott Foresman·Addison Wesley

enVisionMATH®
Common Core

PEARSON

Glenview, Illinois • Boston, Massachusetts • Chandler, Arizona • Upper Saddle River, New Jersey

ISBN-13: 978-0-328-81072-7

ISBN-10: 0-328-81072-X

2 3 4 5 6 7 8 9 10 V0N4 17 16 15 14

Contents

Counting 1, 2, and 3

1

2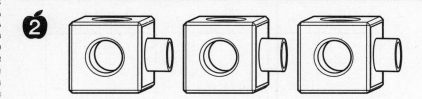

3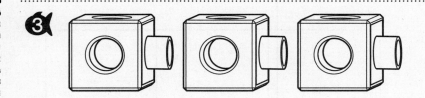

4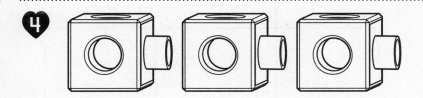

Directions Give each child 3 cubes. Have children choose cubes and color that number of cubes to show how many.
⭐ Choose 2 cubes. **2** Choose 3 cubes. **3** Choose 1 cube. **4** Choose 3 cubes.

Counting 1, 2, and 3

 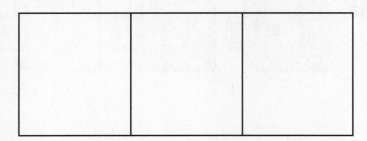

 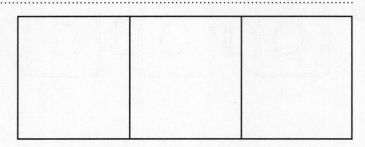

 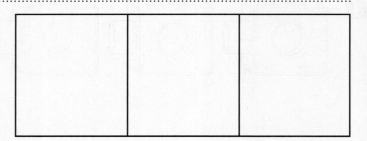

 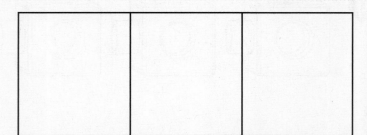

Directions Have children count the animals in each picture and color the correct number of boxes to show how many.

Counting 1, 2, and 3 in Different Arrangements

1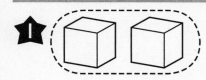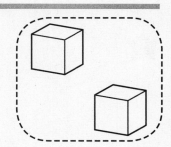

2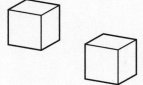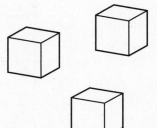

3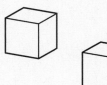

Directions Have children: **1** look at the groups of boxes and trace the circles around the groups with 2 boxes; **2** circle the groups with 3 boxes; **3** circle the groups that show 1 box.

R 1·2

Name _____

Counting 1, 2, and 3 in Different Arrangements

★ 1

🍎 2

◀ 3

Directions Have children count how many birds they see and say the number aloud. Then, have children trace the same number of circles in the boxes and color the boxes to show how many.

Name _____

Reading and Writing 1, 2, and 3

 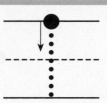  

 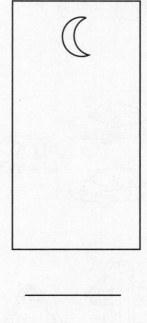

_____ _____ _____

- -

_____ _____ _____

Directions Have children: ★ trace each number; ② count the moons and write the number of moons under each picture.

Name _____

Reading and Writing 1, 2, and 3

1

2

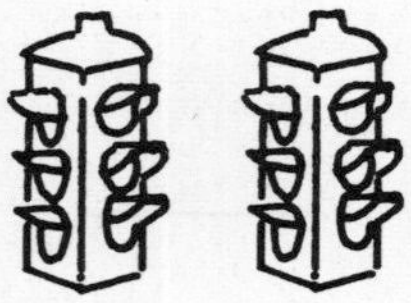

3

4

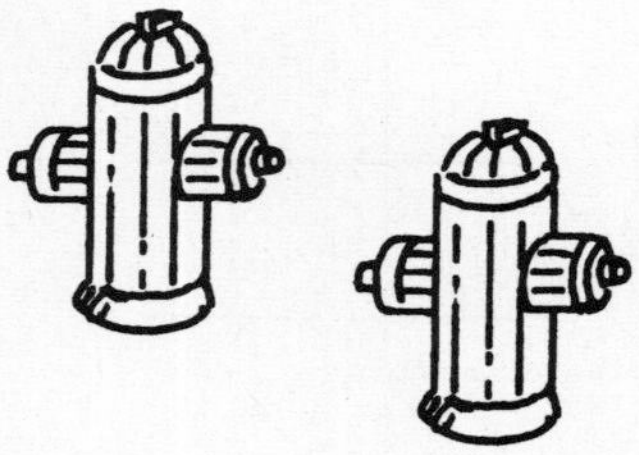

5

Directions Have children count each group and practice writing the number.

Counting 4 and 5

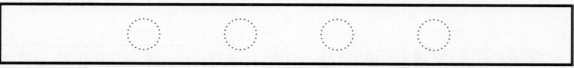

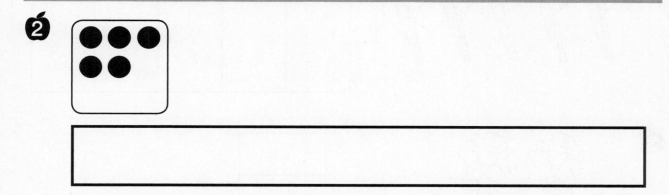

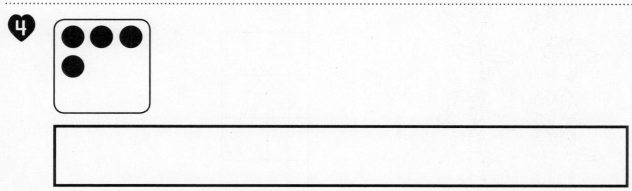

Directions In each exercise, have children count the dots and use counters to show that number. Then have children draw dots in the box to show the same number of dots.

Name _____

Counting 4 and 5

1

2

3

 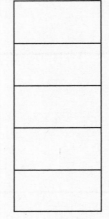

4

Directions Have children count the flowers in each group and color the correct number of boxes to show how many.

P 1·4

Counting 4 and 5 in Different Arrangements

Directions Have children: ⭐ look at the two circled groups that show 4 and color the stars in both groups; 🍎 look at the circled group that shows 5 and circle and color another group that shows 5; 🐟 circle and then color the two groups that show 3.

Counting 4 and 5 in Different Arrangements

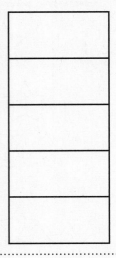

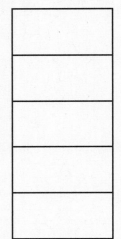

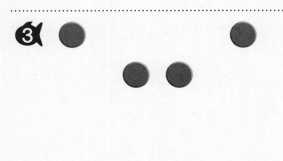

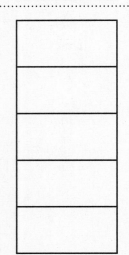

Directions Have children count the counters and say the number aloud. Then, have children draw the same number of circles in the boxes and color the boxes to show how many.

Reading and Writing 4 and 5

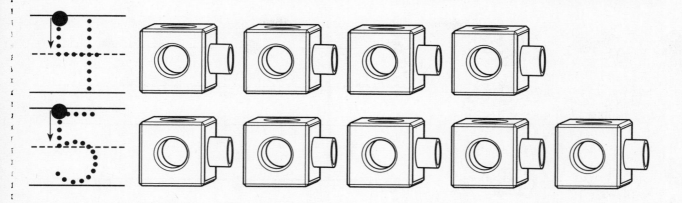

⭐1 _____

② _____

③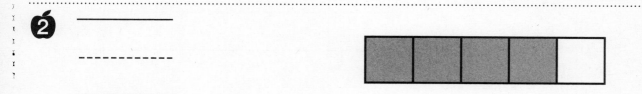

Directions Have children count the cubes and trace each number at the top of the page. Then have children: ⭐1 – ② count the shaded part of the 5-frame, then write the number of boxes shaded next to each frame; ③ practice writing numbers 1 through 5.

Reading and Writing 4 and 5

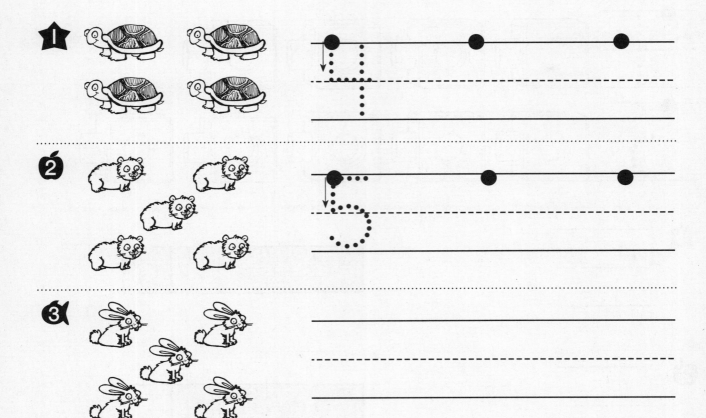

Directions Have children: ⭐–③ count each group and practice writing the number; ④–✋ use counters to show the number. Then have them draw the same number of counters to show how many.

Problem Solving: Use Objects

 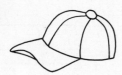 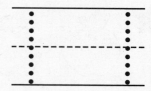

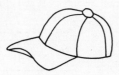  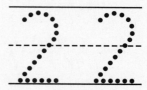

   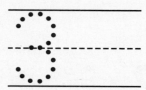

 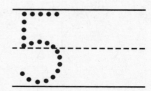

Directions For each row, have children place counters on the hats as they count them. Then have children trace and then write the number.

Problem Solving: Use Objects

1

2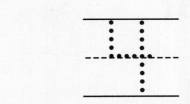

3

4

5

6

Directions Have children place a counter on each picture as they count it. Then have children write the number.

More, Fewer, and Same As

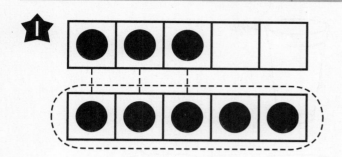

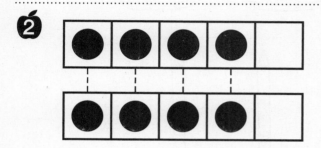

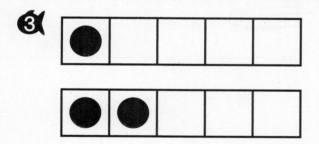

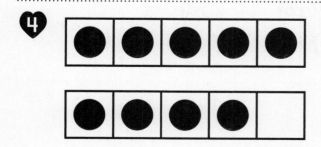

Directions Have children: ⭐ trace a line from each counter in the top frame to a counter in the bottom frame and then trace the circle around the group that has more; 🍎 draw lines and use the term *same number of* to tell about the groups; ❸–❹ draw lines and circle the group that has fewer.

R 2•1

Name _____

More, Fewer, and Same As

1

 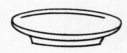 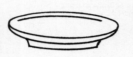 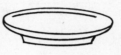

2

   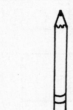 

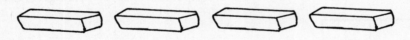

3

4

Directions Have children draw a line from each object in the top row to an object in the bottom row. Then have them circle each group that has fewer. If the groups have the same number of objects, circle the exercise number.

Name _____

I and 2 More

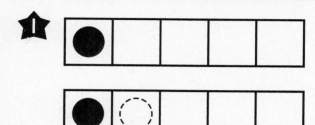

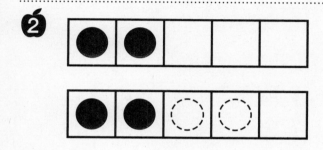

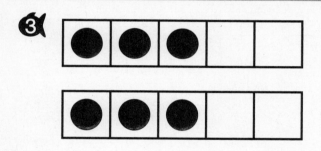

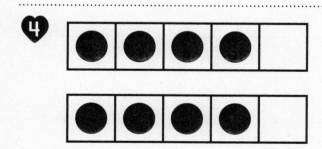

Directions Have children: ⭐–🍎 look at the top frame and show I or 2 more in the bottom frame by tracing circles; ⭐ look at the top frame and draw 2 more in the bottom frame; ❤ look at the top frame and draw I more in the bottom frame. Then have children look at all 4 exercises and circle the groups that show 2 more.

Name _____

I and 2 More

 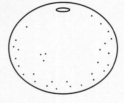 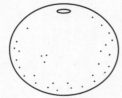 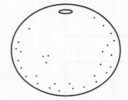

Directions Have children: ★ draw I more banana; ② draw I more sandwich; ③ draw 2 more oranges; ④ draw 2 more muffins. Then have children tell about each row of pictures using the terms *I more* or *2 more*.

Name _____

1 and 2 Fewer

1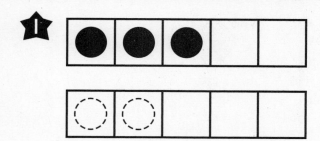

2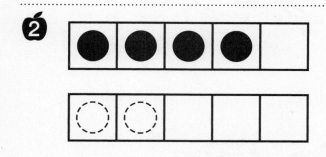

3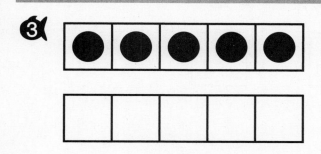

4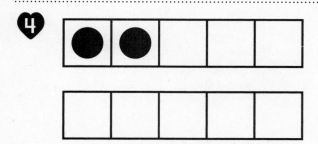

Directions Have children: **1**–**2** look at the top frame and show 1 or 2 fewer in the bottom frame by tracing circles; **3** look at the top frame and draw 2 fewer in the bottom frame; **4** look at the top frame and draw 1 fewer in the bottom frame. Then have children look at all 4 exercises and circle the groups that show 2 fewer.

R 2·3

Name _____

Fewer

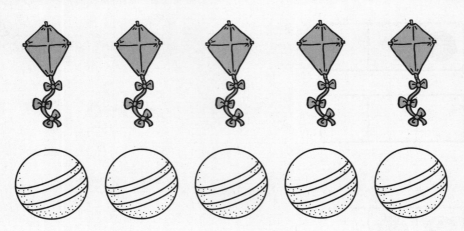

Directions Have children look at the shaded objects and: ⭐ color balls to show 2 fewer; ❷ color shapes to show 1 fewer; ❸ color skateboards to show 1 fewer.

P 2·3

Copyright © Pearson Education, Inc., or its affiliates. All Rights Reserved. K

Name ______________________________

As Many, More, and Fewer

1

2

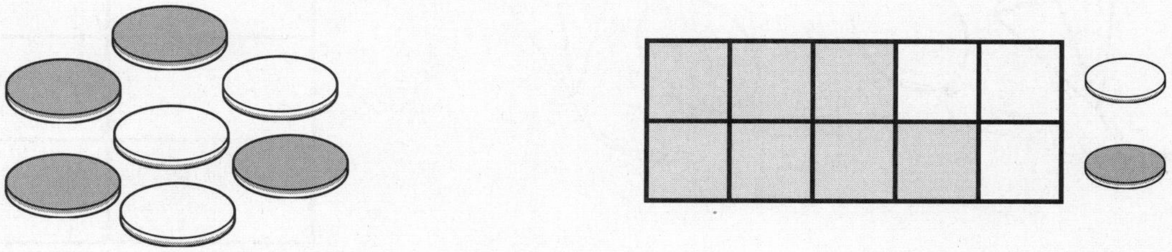

3

4

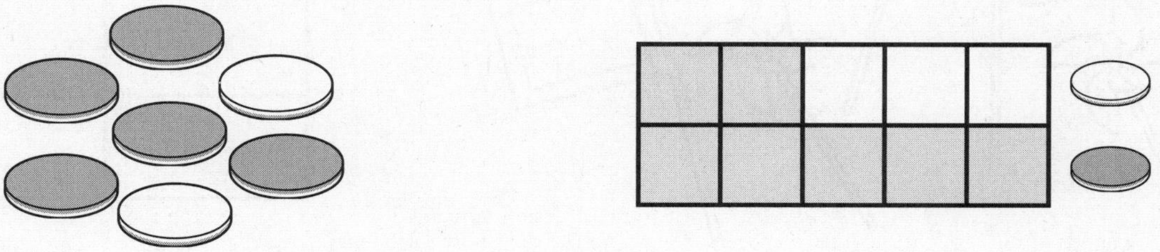

5

Directions *The graphs show the numbers of each colored counter.* Have children: 1 – 2 put a check mark next to the row with more counters; 3 – 5 put a check mark next to the row with fewer counters. If there are the same number of counters, have children add a check mark next to each row.

Name _____

As Many, More, and Fewer

1

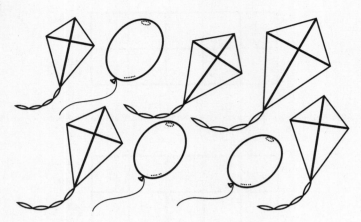

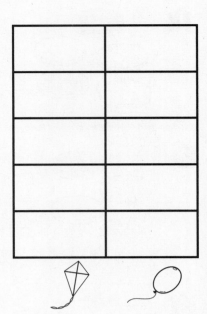

2

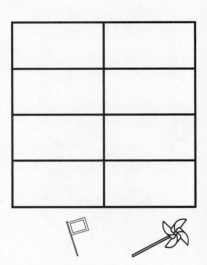

3

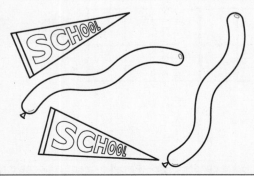

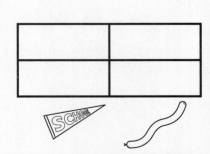

Directions Have children color a box on the graph for each object. Have them circle the picture below the column with fewer objects. If there is the same number of objects, circle the exercise number.

Comparing Numbers Through 5

★ 1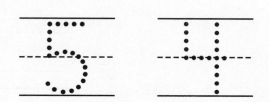

②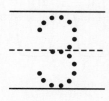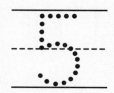

③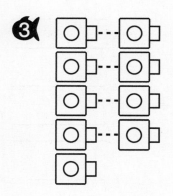

④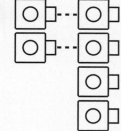

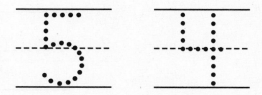

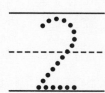 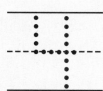

Name _____

Comparing Numbers Through 5

_____

- - - - - - - - - - - -

_____

- - - - - - - - - - - -

_____

- - - - - - - - - - - -

_____

- - - - - - - - - - - -

_____

- - - - - - - - - - - -

_____

- - - - - - - - - - - -

_____

- - - - - - - - - - - -

_____

- - - - - - - - - - - -

Directions Have children draw a line from each item in one group to each item in the other group. Then count each group of objects, write the number, and circle the number that is less.

P 2·5

Name _____

The Number 0

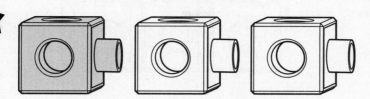

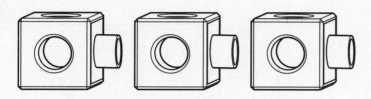

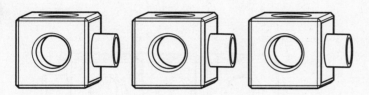

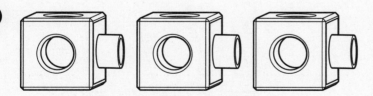

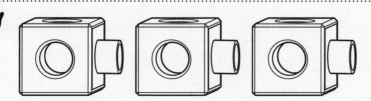

Directions Give each child 3 cubes. Have children choose cubes and color that number of cubes to show how many.
⭐ Choose 1 cube. ❷ Choose 0 cubes. ❸ Choose 2 cubes. ❹ Choose 0 cubes. ✋ Choose 3 cubes.

Name _____

The Number 0

  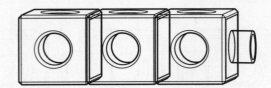

 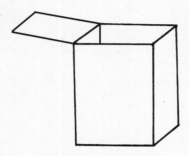 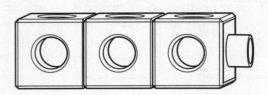

  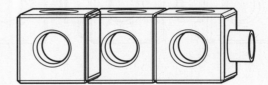

 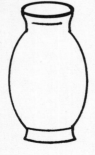 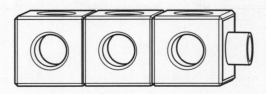

Directions Have children count the objects in each container and then color the correct number of cubes to show how many objects.

Name _____

Reading and Writing 0

⭐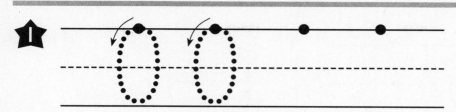

② _____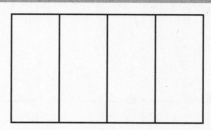

③ _____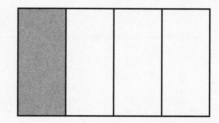

④ _____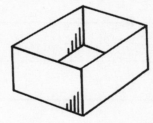

✋ _____

Directions Have children: ⭐ practice writing the number 0; ②–③ count how many shaded boxes and write the matching number; ④ write the number that tells how many balls are in the box; ✋ write the number that tells how many crayons are in the hand.

Name _____

Reading and Writing 0

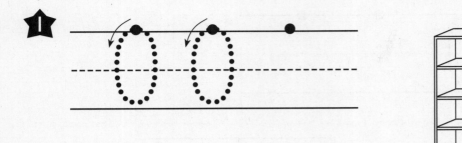

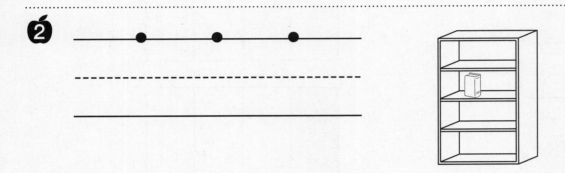

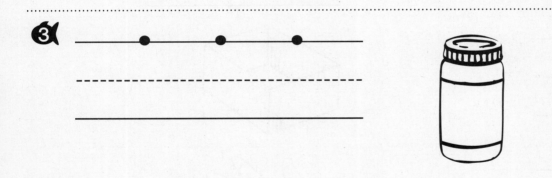

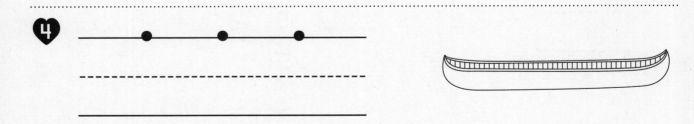

Directions Have children: ❶–❷ count the number of books on the shelves and then practice writing the number that tells how many books; ❸ count the number of marbles in the jar and then practice writing the number that tells how many marbles; ❹ count the number of people in the canoe and then practice writing the number that tells how many people.

Name _____

Ordering Numbers 0 to 5

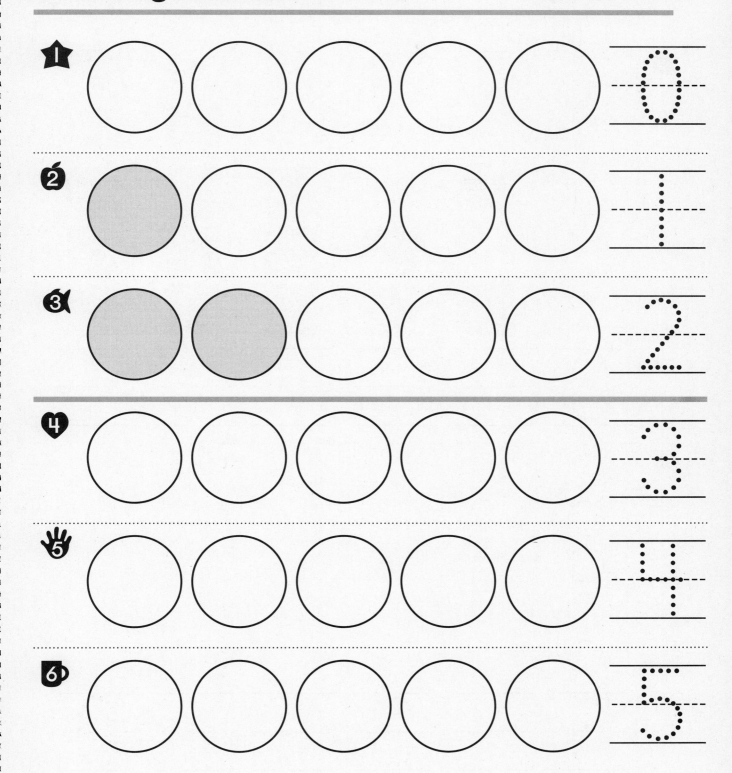

Directions Have children use counters to show each number and then color to show the number. Then have them trace the number, count aloud from 0 to 5, and then count aloud backward from 5 to 0.

Ordering Numbers 0 to 5

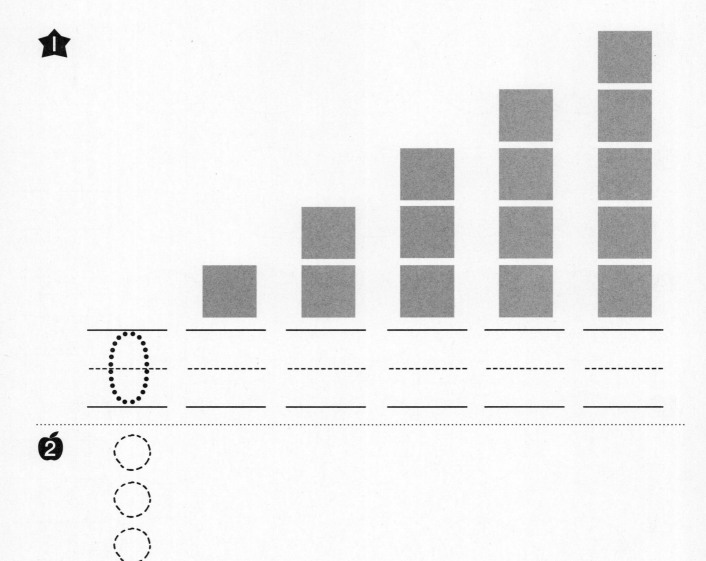

Directions Have children: ⭐ write numbers to show the number of shaded shapes in order from 0 to 5. 🍎 Have children tell a story about eating crackers, one at a time, until none are left. Then have them show what happened in the story by drawing the crackers in order and writing the missing numbers.

Name _____

Problem Solving: Use Objects

①

B	3
R	1
G	5

- - - 1 - - -   - - - 3 - - -   - - - 5 - - -

②

Y	2
R	3
B	1

_____   _____   _____

- - - - - -   - - - - - -   - - - - - -

Directions Have children listen to each story and write the numbers in order below. **①** *Shea has 3 blue tiles, 1 red tile, and 5 green tiles. Which group has the fewest?* Draw a box around the number that tells which group has the fewest. **②** *Mollie has 2 yellow marbles, 3 red marbles, and 1 blue marble. Which group has the most?* Circle the number that tells which group has the most.

Name _____

Problem Solving: Use Objects

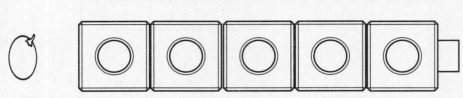

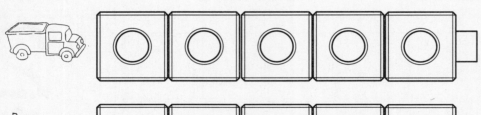

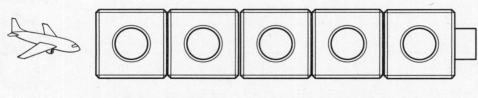

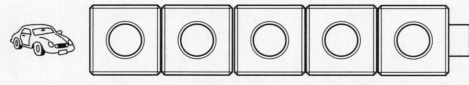

Directions Have children listen to each story, color to show the number of cubes in each group, and then write the number for each group. Then have them write the number of cubes in order below from fewest to most. ⭐ *Angel has 2 apples, 1 orange, and 4 grapes. Which group has the most?* Circle the number that tells which group has the most. ② *Shon has 4 toy trucks, 2 toy planes, and 5 toy cars. Which group has the fewest?* Draw a box around the number that tells which group has the fewest.

Name _____

Counting 6 and 7

Directions In each exercise, have children count the dots and use counters to show that number. Then have them draw dots in the empty box to show how many dots.

Name _____

Counting 6 and 7

1

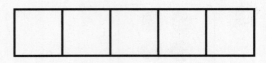

2

3

4

Directions Have children count the birds and then draw the correct number of counters to show how many.

Name _____

Reading and Writing 6 and 7

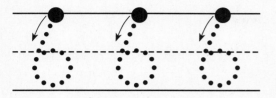

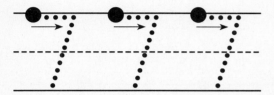

1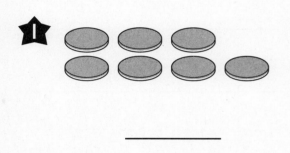

_____

- - - - - - - - -

_____

2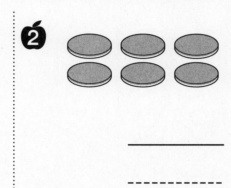

_____

- - - - - - - - -

_____

3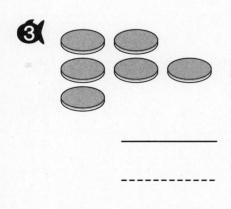

_____

- - - - - - - - -

_____

4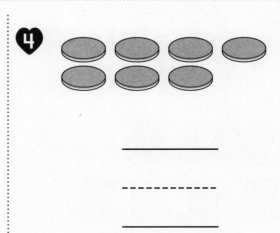

_____

- - - - - - - - -

_____

Directions Have children count the objects and practice writing each number at the top of the page beginning with each black dot. Then have them count the objects in each group and write the number.

Name _____

Reading and Writing 6 and 7

1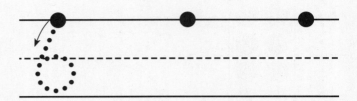

2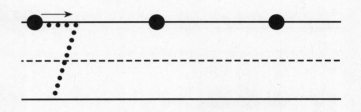

3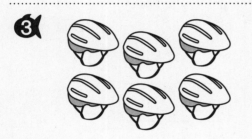

4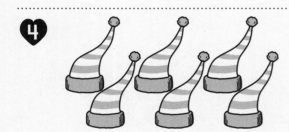

5

Directions Have children count each group and practice writing the number.

Counting 8 and 9

1

2

3

4

Directions In each exercise, have children count the dots and use counters to show that number. Then have them draw dots in the empty box to show how many dots.

Name _____

Counting 8 and 9

    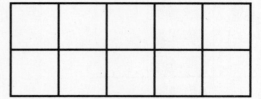

   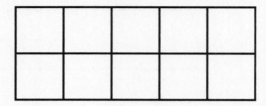

 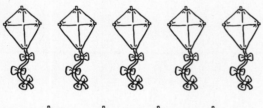   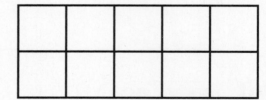

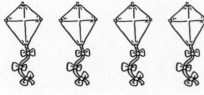

 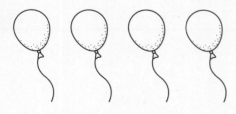   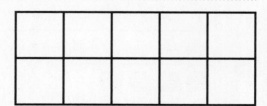

Directions Have children count the objects in each group and draw the correct number of counters to show how many.

Name _____

Reading and Writing 8 and 9

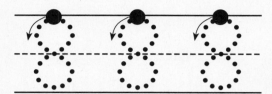

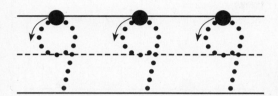

★1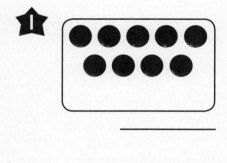

_____

- - - - - - - - - - -

_____

🍎2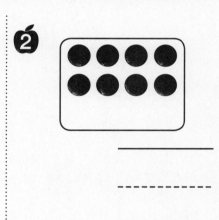

_____

- - - - - - - - - - -

_____

3

4

Directions Have children count the objects and practice writing each number at the top of the page beginning with the black dot. Have children: **1–2** count the objects in each group and write the number; **3–4** use counters to show the number. Then have them draw the same number of counters to show how many.

Reading and Writing 8 and 9

1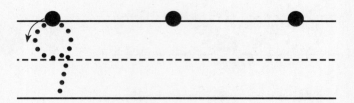

2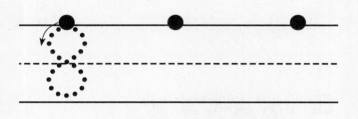

3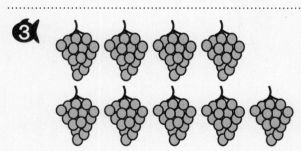

4

5

Name _____

Counting 10

 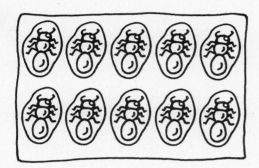 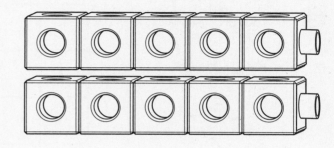

❷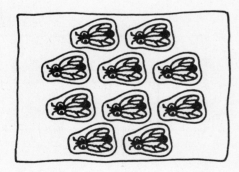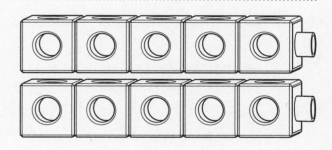

❸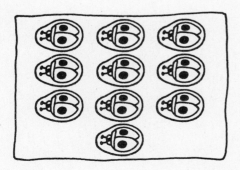

Directions For each exercise, have children count the number of insects and use cubes to show that number. Have children: ❶–❷ color in the cubes to show 10; ❸ use cubes to count and then draw their own cubes to show 10.

R 3·5

Name _____

Counting 10

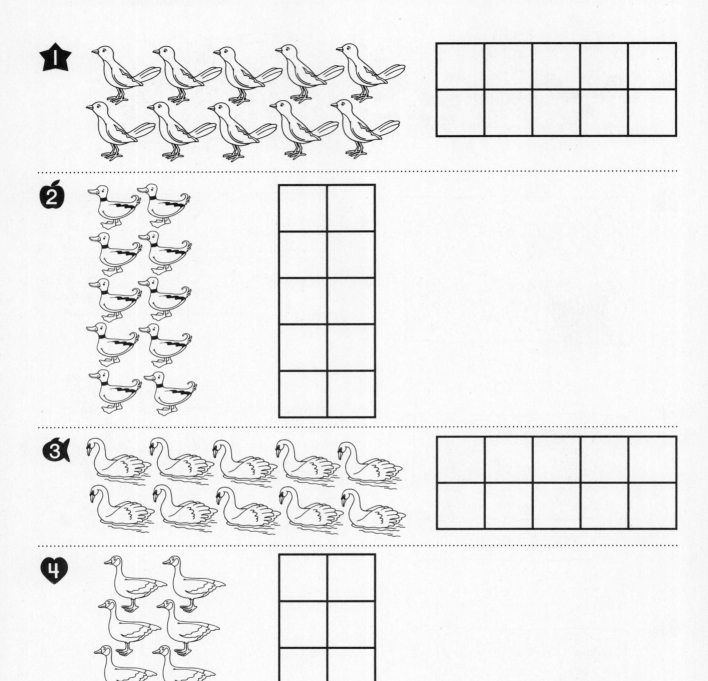

Directions Have children count the animals in each picture, and draw the correct number of counters to show how many.

Name _____

Reading and Writing 10

 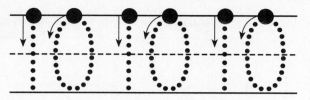 

_____   _____   _____

- - - - - - - - - -   - - - - - - - - - -   - - - - - - - - - -

_____   _____   _____

Directions Have children: ① count the stars and practice writing 10 beginning with each black dot; ② count each group of stars and write the number of stars under each group.

R 3·6

Reading and Writing 10

1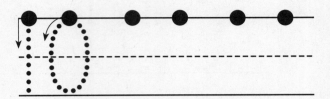

2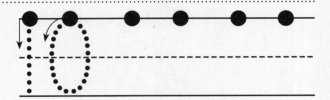

3

4

Directions Have children count the objects in each group and practice writing the number 10.

Problem Solving: Look for a Pattern

1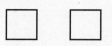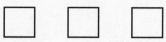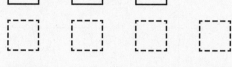

2

3

Directions Have children draw 1 or 2 more rows of shapes to show what comes next in the pattern.

Problem Solving: Look for a Pattern

⭐ 1

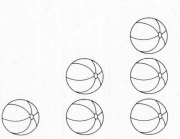

🍎 2

3

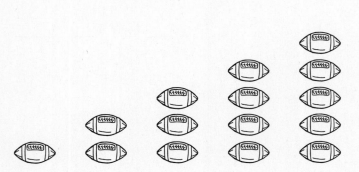

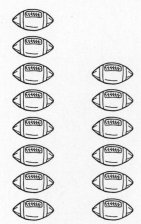

Directions Have children circle the set of pictures that shows what comes next in the pattern.

Comparing Numbers Through 10

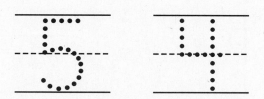

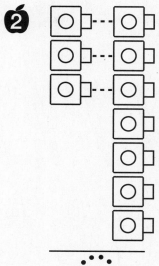

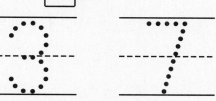

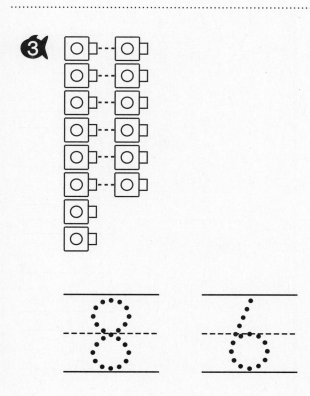

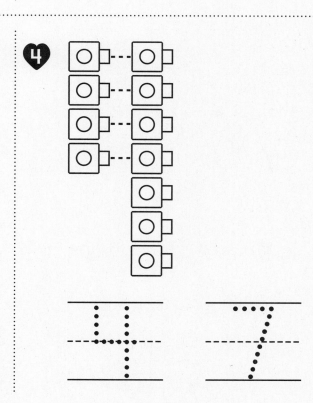

Directions Have children: ★–🍎 trace a line from each cube in the first column to each cube in the next column, and count and trace each number; then circle the number that is greater; ★–❤ repeat and then circle the number that is less.

Name _____

Comparing Numbers Through 10

1

_____

- - - - - - - - - - - - - -

_____

- - - - - - - - - - - - - -

_____

- - - - - - - - - - - - - -

2

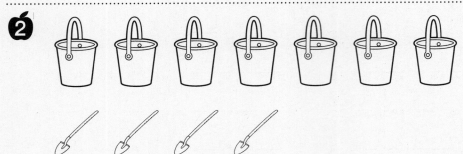

_____

- - - - - - - - - - - - - -

_____

- - - - - - - - - - - - - -

3

_____

- - - - - - - - - - - - - -

_____

- - - - - - - - - - - - - -

4

_____

- - - - - - - - - - - - - -

_____

- - - - - - - - - - - - - -

_____

Directions Have children draw a line from each item in one group to each item in the other group. Then count and write the number and circle the number that is less.

Comparing Numbers to 5

 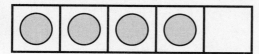 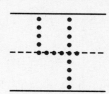

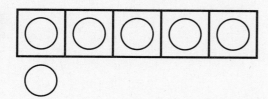 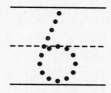

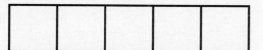 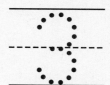

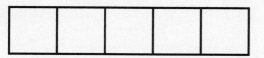 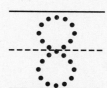

Directions Have children: ⭐ — 🍎 color the counters to show the number, trace the number, and then circle the number if it is greater than 5; 🎣 — ❤️ draw counters to show the number, trace the number, and circle it if it is greater than 5.

Name _____

Comparing Numbers to 5

_____

- - - - - - - - -

_____

_____

- - - - - - - - -

_____

---

❸

_____

- - - - - - - - -

_____

---

❹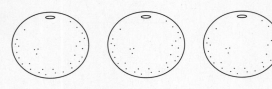

_____

- - - - - - - - -

_____

Directions Have children count how many and write the number. Then have children circle the number if it is less than 5.

Name _____

Comparing Numbers to 10

 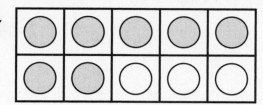

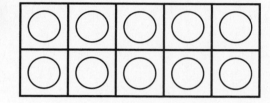

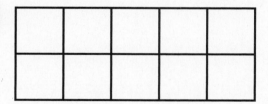

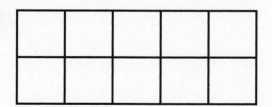

Directions Have children: ❶ – ❷ color the counters to show a number that is less than 10; ❸ – ❹ draw counters to show a number that is greater than 10.

Name _____

Comparing Numbers to 10

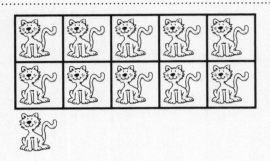

Directions Have children circle each picture that shows fewer than 10.

I More

 1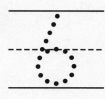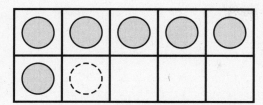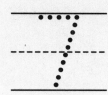

2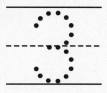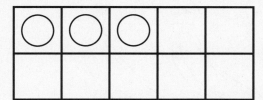

3

4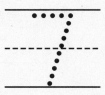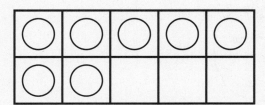

Directions Have children trace the number and color the counters to show that number. Then have them draw a counter to show 1 more and write the number that tells 1 more.

Name _____

I More

1

_____

- - - - - - - - -

_____

2

_____

- - - - - - - - -

_____

3

_____

- - - - - - - - -

_____

4

_____

- - - - - - - - -

_____

Directions Have children draw I more piece of fruit and then write the number that tells I more.

Name _____

1 Fewer

 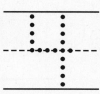 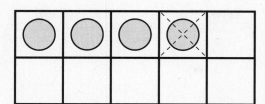 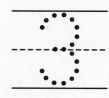

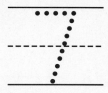 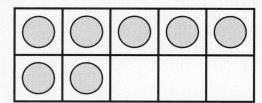

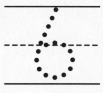 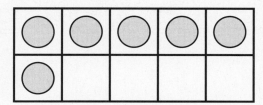

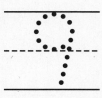 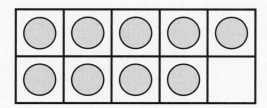 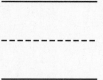

Directions Have children count the counters and trace the number. Then have them mark an X on 1 counter to show 1 fewer and write the number that tells 1 fewer.

Name _____

I Fewer

_____
- - - - - - - - - - -
_____

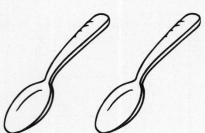

_____
- - - - - - - - - - -
_____

_____
- - - - - - - - - - -
_____

_____
- - - - - - - - - - -
_____

Directions Have children mark an X on I object to show I fewer and then write the number that tells I fewer.

2 More

 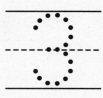 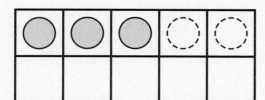 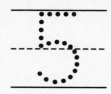

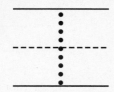

 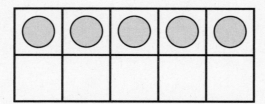

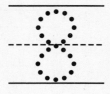 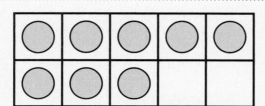

Directions Have children trace the number and color the counters to show that number. Then have them draw counters to show 2 more and write the number that tells 2 more.

Name _____

2 More

1

_____
- - - - - - - - - -
_____

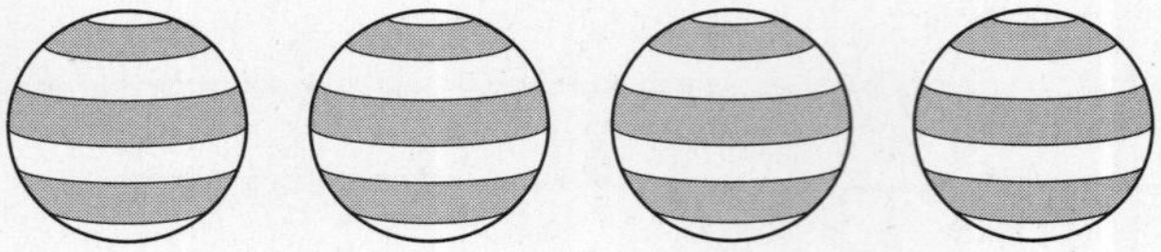

2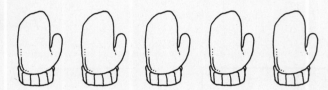

_____
- - - - - - - - - -
_____

3

_____
- - - - - - - - - -
_____

4

_____
- - - - - - - - - -
_____

Directions Have children draw 2 more objects and then write the number that tells 2 more.

P 4·6

2 Fewer

 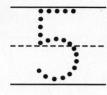 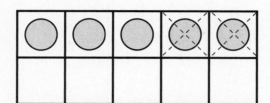 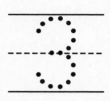

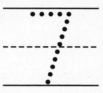 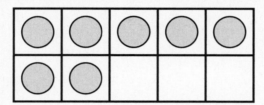

 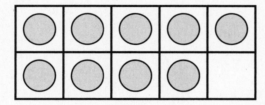

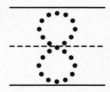 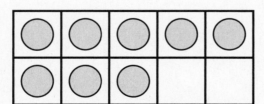

Directions Have children count the counters and trace the number. Then have them mark Xs on 2 counters to show 2 fewer and write the number that tells 2 fewer.

Name _____

2 Fewer

1

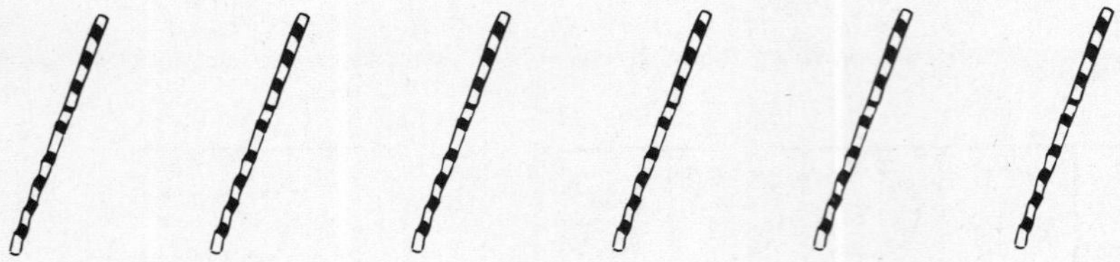

2

3

4

5

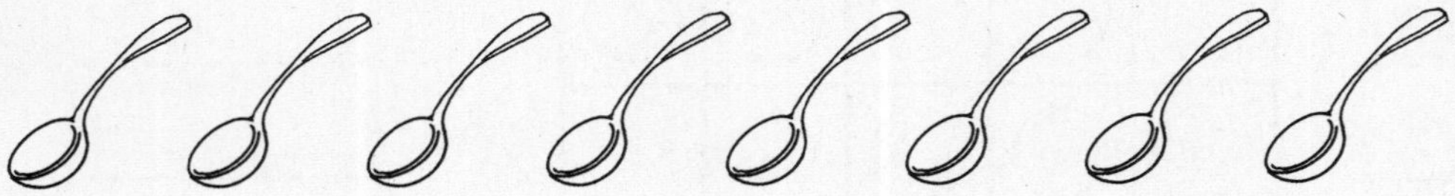

Directions Have children mark an X on 2 objects to show 2 fewer and then write the number that tells 2 fewer.

Name _____

Ordering Numbers Through 10

   8   9

10 5 7 6 2

0 1

6

Directions Have children use the number cards to order the numbers 0 to 10. Have children find the card with 0, mark an X on it, and then trace the number below. Repeat for the number 1. Have children continue until they write all the numbers in order. Then have them read the numbers they wrote to count in order from 0 to 10.

R 4·8

Name _____

Ordering Numbers Through 10

1 ⭐ | 5 | | 8 | | 7 | | 6 |

_____ _____ _____ _____

- -

_____ _____ _____ _____

2 🍎 | 4 | | 6 | | 3 | | 5 |

_____ _____ _____ _____

- -

_____ _____ _____ _____

3 🐟 | 9 | | 6 | | 8 | | 7 |

_____ _____ _____ _____

- -

_____ _____ _____ _____

4 ❤️ | 10 | | 7 | | 8 | | 9 |

_____ _____ _____ _____

- -

_____ _____ _____ _____

5 ✋ | 7 | | 4 | | 6 | | 5 |

_____ _____ _____ _____

- -

_____ _____ _____ _____

Directions Have children write the numbers in the correct order.

Using a Number Line

1

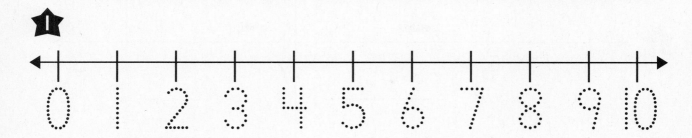

2

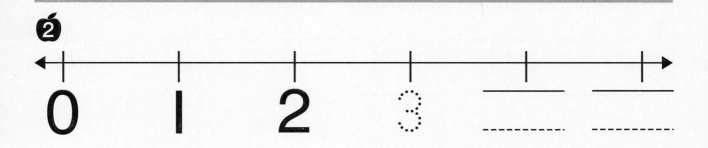

3

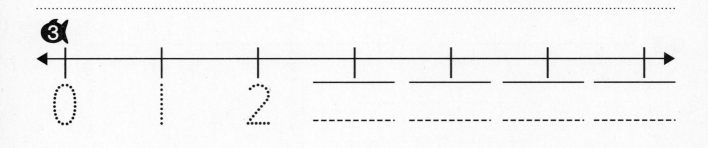

4

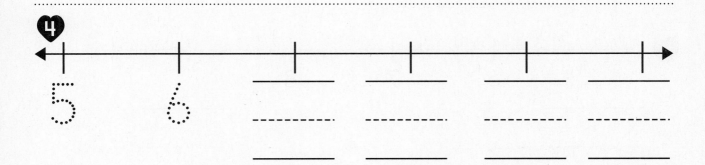

Directions Have children count as they trace or write the missing numbers to complete the number lines.

R 4·9

Name _____

Using a Number Line

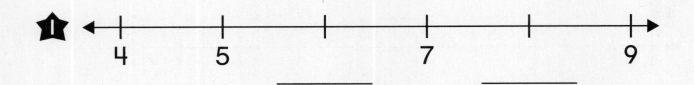

1 4   5   7   9

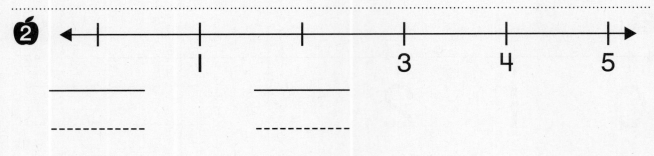

2 1   3   4   5

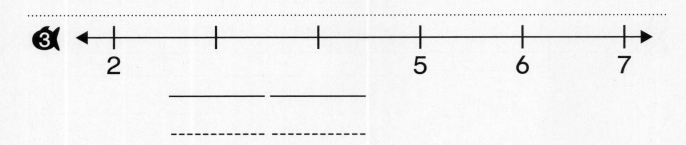

3 2   5   6   7

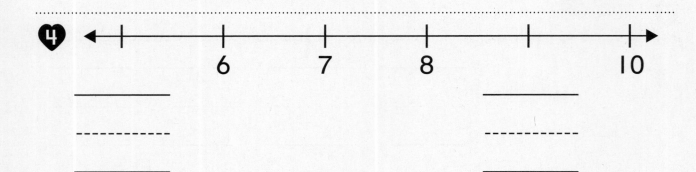

4 6   7   8   10

Directions Have children write the missing numbers in each number line.

Name _____

Problem Solving: Use Objects

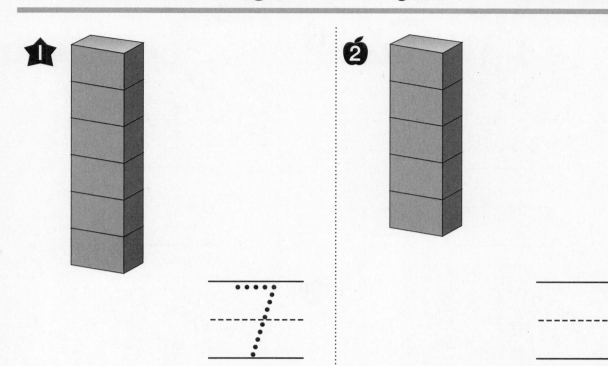

⭐ 1

🍎 2

7

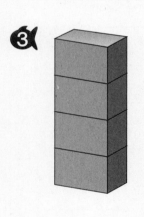

🐟 3

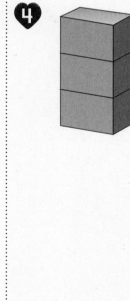

❤ 4

Directions *One child builds a tower. Her partner adds 1 more block to the tower. How many blocks now make up the tower? How can we find out?* Have children: ⭐1 – 🍎2 *add a counter (to represent a block) to each tower, count the total and write the number to show 1 more;* 🐟3 – ❤4 *use counters to show 2 more and write the number.*

R 4·10

Problem Solving: Use Objects

_____

- - - - - - - - - -

_____

_____

- - - - - - - - - -

_____

_____

- - - - - - - - - -

_____

_____

- - - - - - - - - -

_____

_____

- - - - - - - - - -

_____

Directions _Nina sees butterflies in a bush. Then she sees 2 more. How many butterflies are there now?_ Have children use counters and explain their answers. Then have them write the number.

Counting, Reading, and Writing 11 and 12

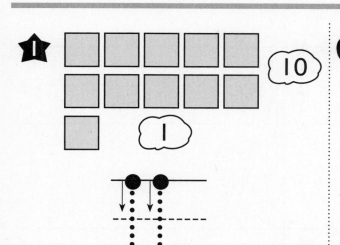

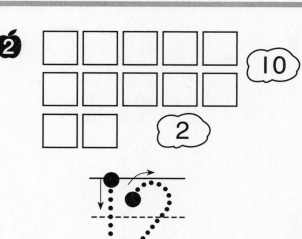

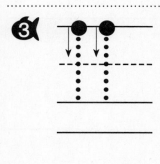

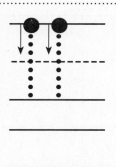

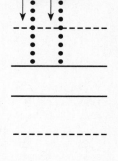

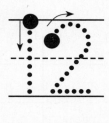

Directions Have children: ⭐ – 🍎 count the squares, color the number shown, and trace the number; 🐟 – ❤️ practice writing the numbers.

Counting, Reading, and Writing 11 and 12

1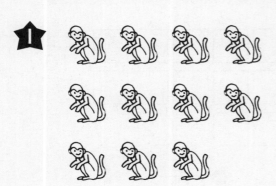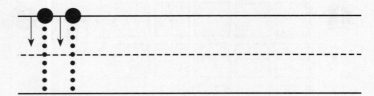

2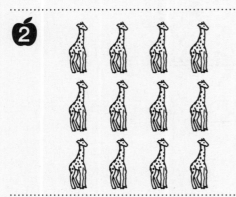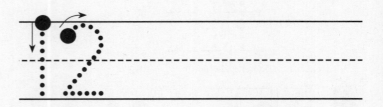

3

4

Directions Have children count each group and practice writing the numbers.

Counting, Reading, and Writing 13, 14, and 15

⭐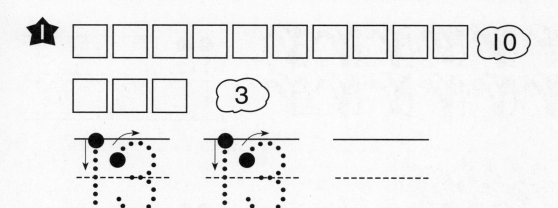

❷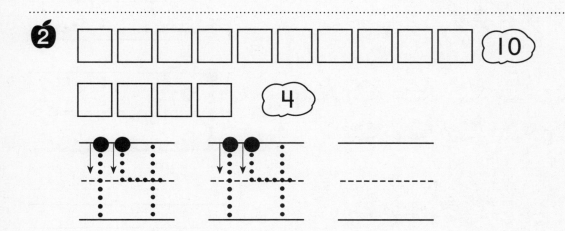

❸

Directions Have children count the squares and practice writing the number.

Name ______________________________

Practice
5-2

Counting, Reading, and Writing 13, 14, and 15

1

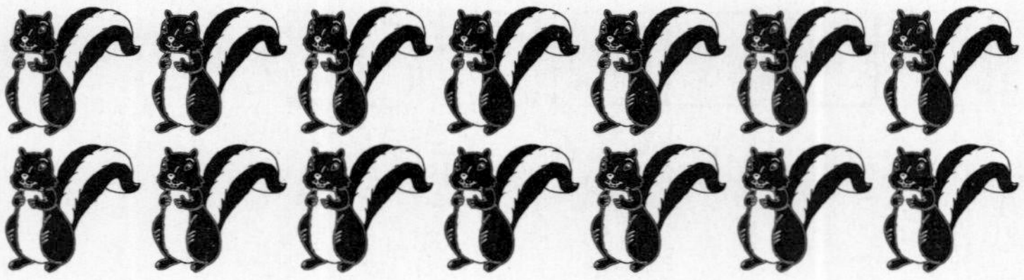

14 14

2

15 15

3

13 13

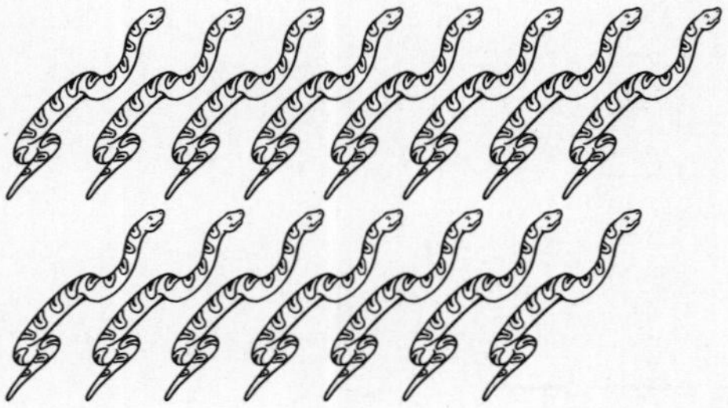

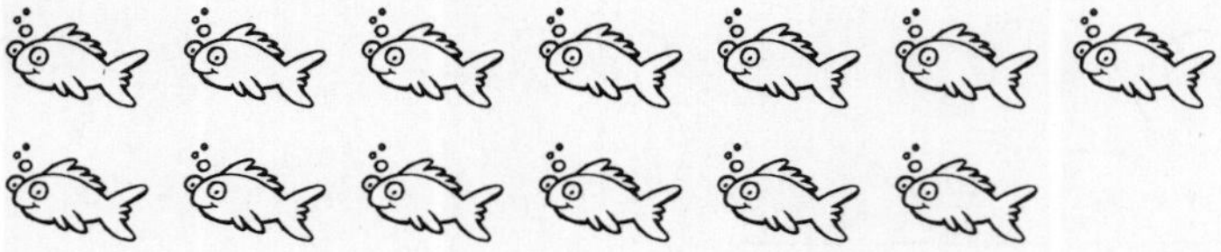

4

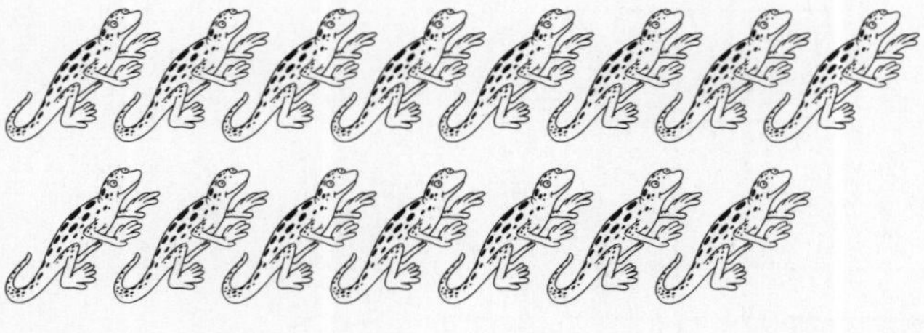

5

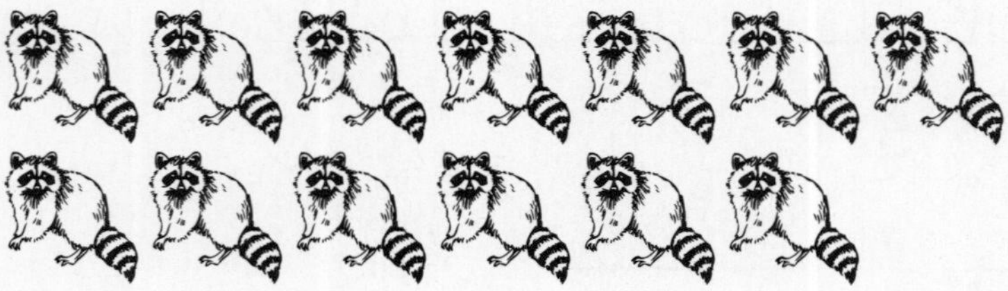

Directions In each row have children count the animals and practice writing the numbers.

Counting, Reading, and Writing 16 and 17

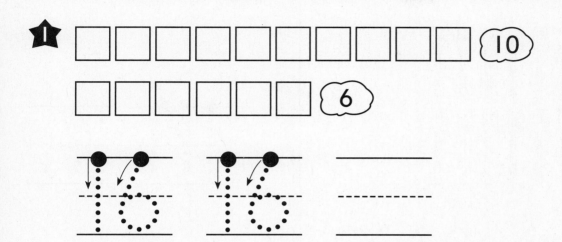

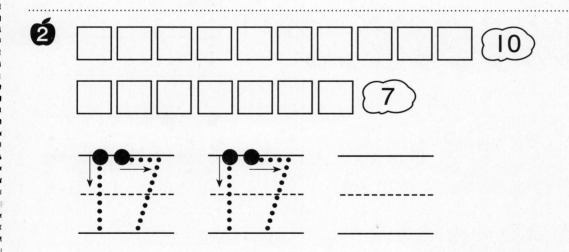

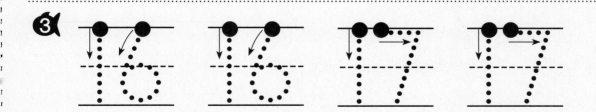

Directions Have children: ★-② count the squares and practice writing the number; ③ trace the numbers.

Counting, Reading, and Writing 16 and 17

1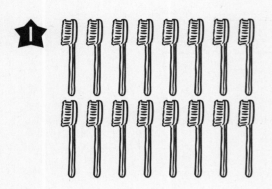

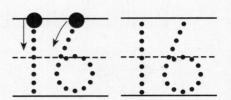

2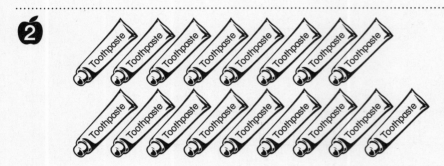

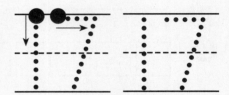

3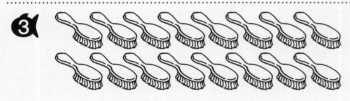

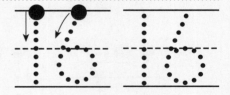

4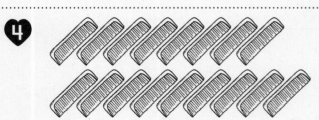

_____ _____

- - - - - - - - - - - - - - - - - - - - - - - -

_____ _____

5

_____ _____

- - - - - - - - - - - - - - - - - - - - - - - -

_____ _____

Directions In each row have children count the objects and practice writing the numbers.

Counting, Reading, and Writing 18, 19, and 20

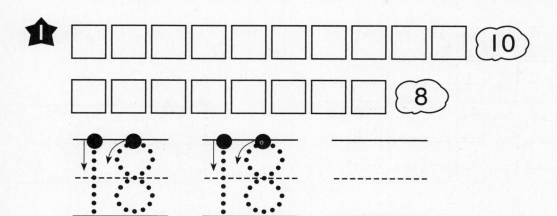

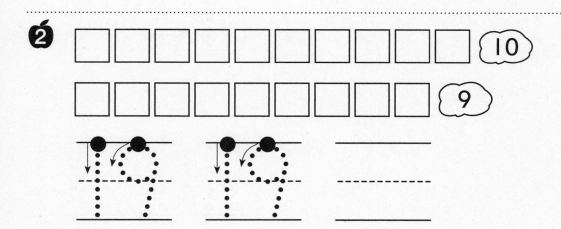

Directions Have children count the boxes and practice writing the number.

Counting, Reading, and Writing 18, 19, and 20

1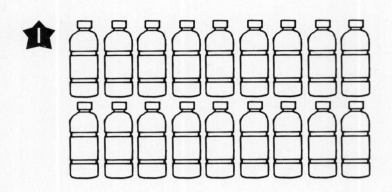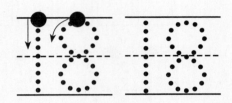

2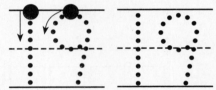

3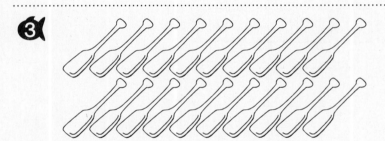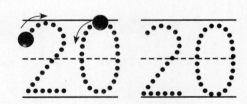

4

5

Directions In each row have children count the objects and practice writing the numbers.

How Many?

1

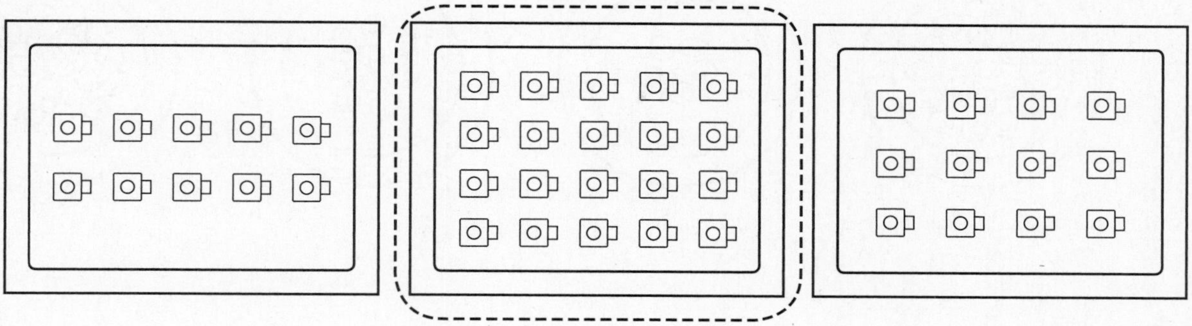

2

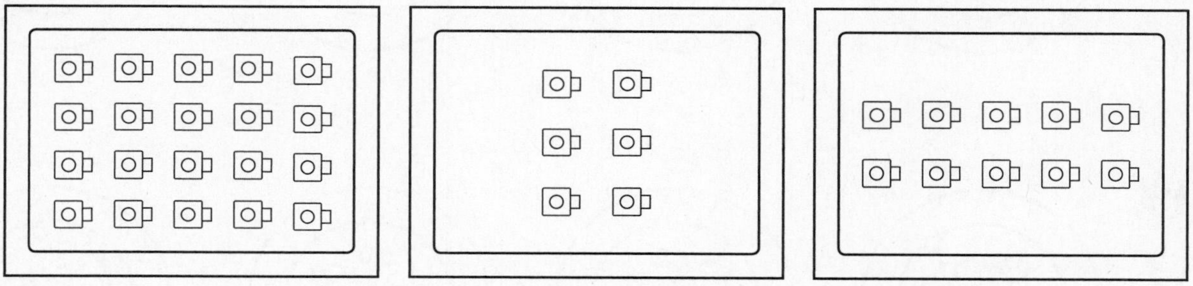

3

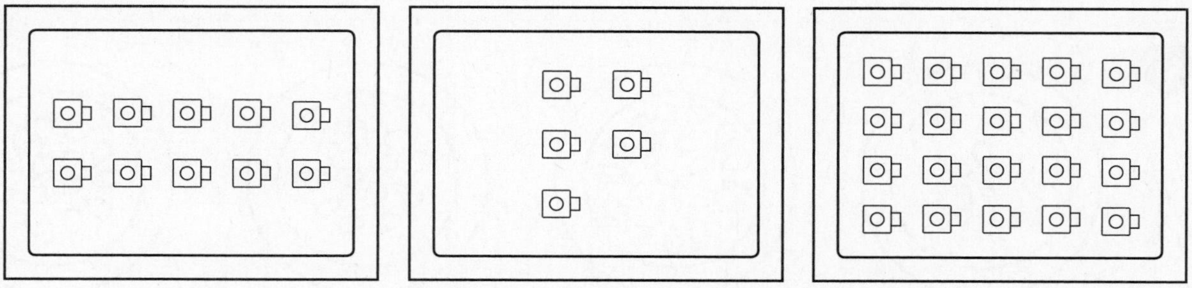

Directions Have children: **1** circle the mat with 20 cubes on it; **2** circle the mat with 10 cubes on it; **3** circle the mat with 5 cubes on it.

Name _____

How Many?

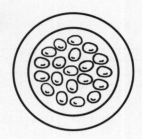 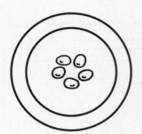 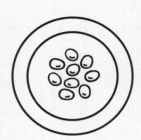 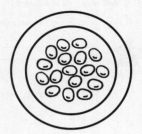

  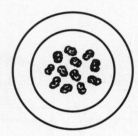 

  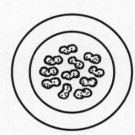 

  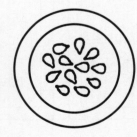 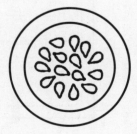

Directions Have children: ❶ circle the plate with 9 grapes on it; ❷ circle the plate with 6 raisins on it; ❸ circle the plate with 11 peanuts on it; ❹ circle the plate with 12 seeds on it.

Name _____

Problem Solving:
Use Logical Reasoning

1
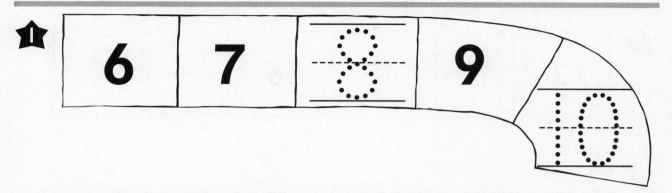

6	7	8	9	10

2
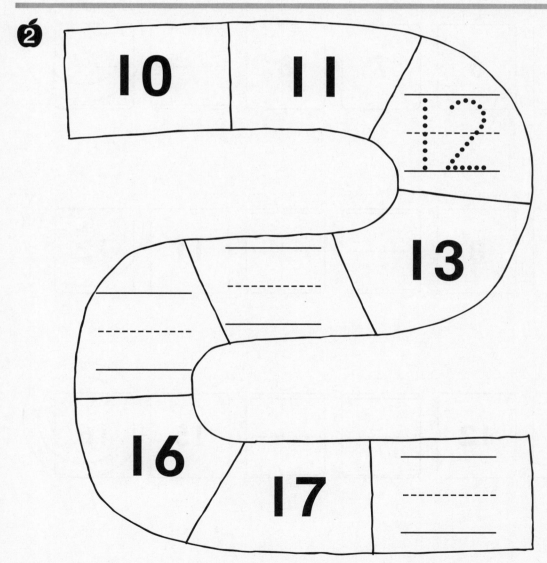

Directions Have children: **1**–**2** write the missing numbers to solve this problem: *Look at the numbers on the game board. How can we find the missing numbers? Describe what you notice about each number as you count forward.*

Problem Solving:
Use Logical Reasoning

1

| 13 | 14 | 15 | 16 | _____ | _____ |

2

| 5 | 6 | 7 | 8 | _____ | _____ |

3

| 7 | 8 | _____ | _____ | 11 | 12 |

4

| 11 | 12 | _____ | _____ | 15 | 16 |

Directions *Look at each row of numbers. How can we find the missing numbers?* Have children identify and write the missing numbers. Have them describe what they notice about each number as they count forward.

Counting to 30

 1

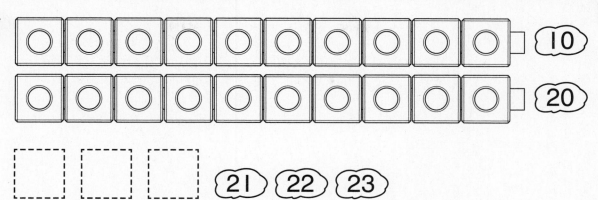

2

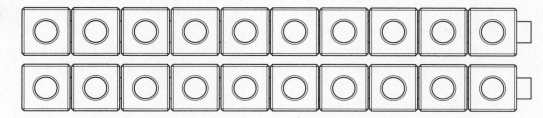

3

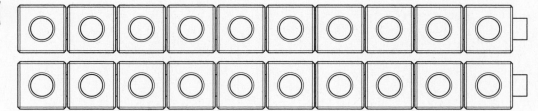

Directions Have children: ❶ trace cubes to show 23 cubes in all; ❷ draw cubes to show 21 cubes in all; ❸ draw cubes to show 26 cubes in all. Children can use cubes as needed.

Name _____

Counting to 30

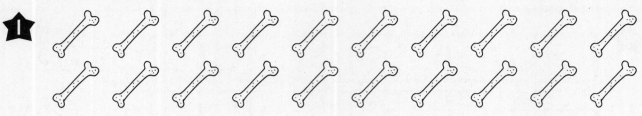

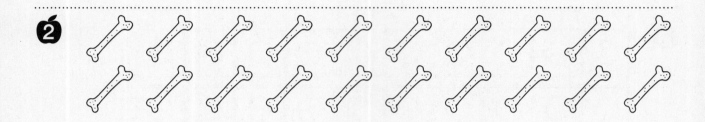

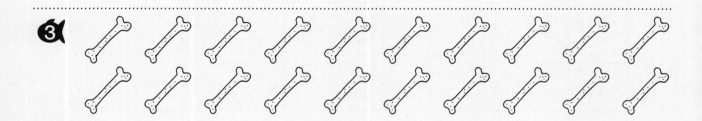

Directions Have children: ❶ count and draw to show 22 dog bones; ❷ count and draw to show 24 dog bones; ❸ count and draw to show 29 dog bones.

Counting to 100

1	2	3	4	5	6	7	8	9	10
11	12	13	14	15	16	17	18	19	20
21	22	23	24	25	26	27	28	29	30
31	32	33	34		36	37	38	39	
41		43	44	45		47	48	49	50
51		53	54		56		58	59	60
61	62	63			66	67	68	69	
71	72			75	76	77		79	80
	82	83	84		86	87	88		90
91	92	93			96	97		99	100

Directions Have children count to 100 and then trace or write the missing numbers.

Name _____

Counting to 100

1	2	3	4	5	6	7	8	9	10
11	12	13	14	15	16	17	18	19	20
21	22	23		25	26		28	29	30
	32	33	34	35	36	37	38		40
41		43	44	45		47	48	49	50
51	52		54		56	57	58	59	60
61		63	64	65	66	67	68	69	
71	72			75	76	77	78	79	80
81	82	83	84			87	88	89	90
91		93	94	95	96	97		99	100

Directions Have children count to 100 on the hundred chart and write the missing numbers.

Counting Groups of Ten

1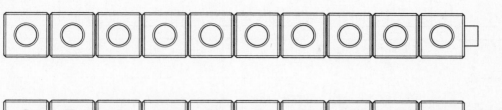

2

3

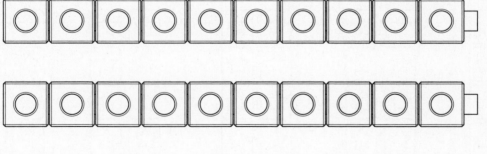

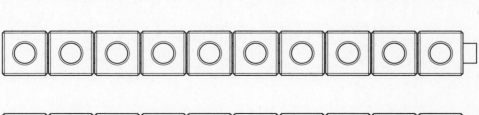

Directions Have children count by groups of 10 and write the numbers.

Name _____

Counting Groups of Ten

❶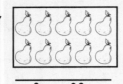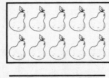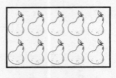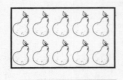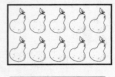

10   20   _____   _____   _____

❷

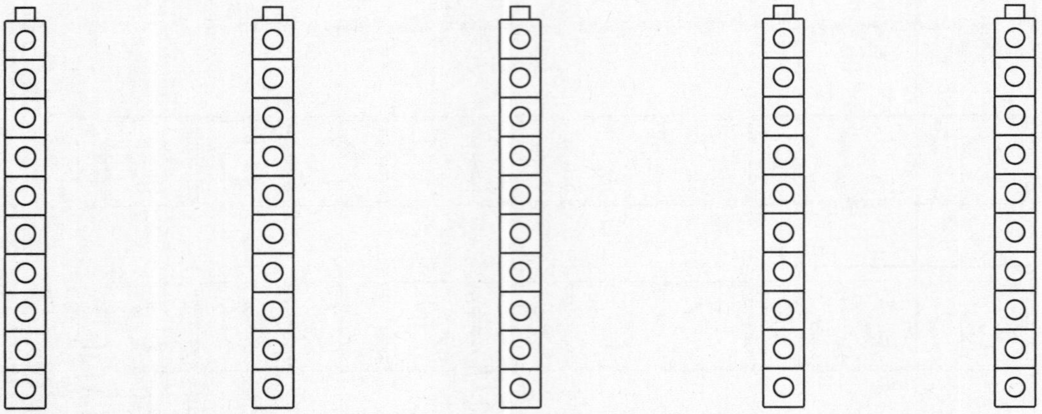

10   _____   _____   _____   _____

❸

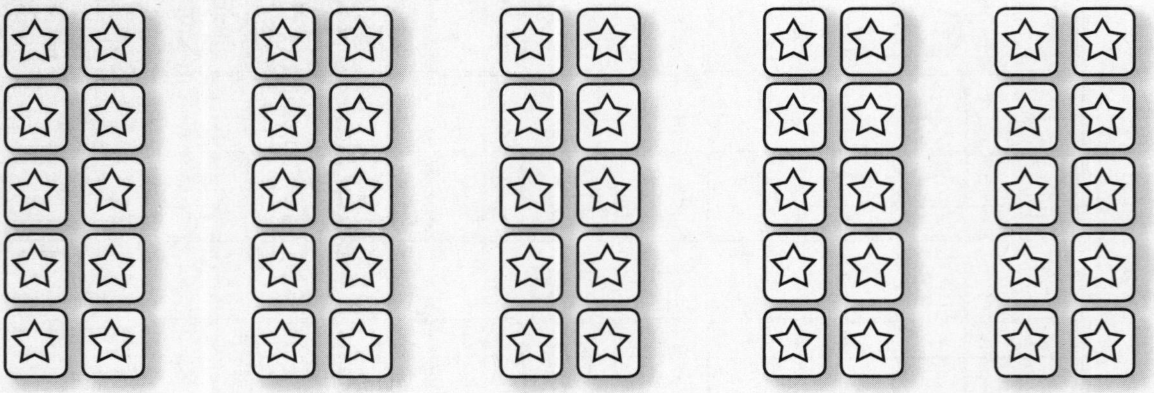

_____   20   _____   _____   _____

Directions In each exercise have children count the groups of 10 and write the numbers.

Name _____

Patterns on a Hundred Chart

1	2	3	4	5	6	7	8	9	10
11	12	13	14	15	16	17	18	19	20
21	22	23	24	25	26	27	28	29	30
31	32	33	34	35	36	37	38	39	40
41	42	43	44	45	46	47	48	49	50
51	52	53	54	55	56	57	58	59	60
61	62	63	64	65	66	67	68	69	70
71	72	73	74	75	76	77	78	79	80
81	82	83	84	85	86	87	88	89	90
91	92	93	94	95	96	97	98	99	100

Directions Have children count by 1s to 10 and color the numbers yellow. Then ask children to use the hundred chart to count aloud by 10s starting with 10 and mark an X on these numbers in blue.

R 6·4

Patterns on a Hundred Chart

1	2	3	4	5	6	7	8	9	10
11	12	13	14	15	16	17	18	19	20
21	22	23	24	25	26	27	28	29	
31	32	33	34	35	36	37	38	39	
41	42	43	44	45	46	47	48	49	
51	52	53	54	55	56	57	58	59	
61	62	63	64	65	66	67	68	69	
71	72	73	74	75	76	77	78	79	
81	82	83	84	85	86	87	88	89	
91	92	93	94	95	96	97	98	99	

Directions Have children write the missing numbers on the hundred chart. Then have children count by 10s starting at 10 and use a red crayon to circle the numbers they counted.

Name _____

Problem Solving:
Look for a Pattern

⭐ 1

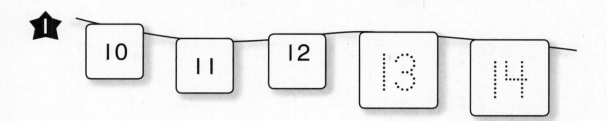

10   11   12   13   14

② 2

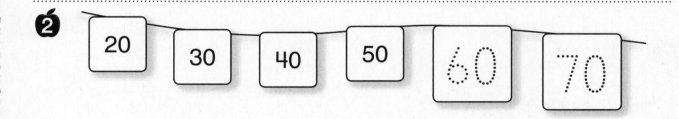

20   30   40   50   60   70

③ 3

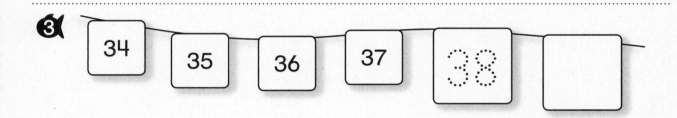

34   35   36   37   38

♥ 4

40   50   60   70

Directions *Look at each row of numbers. How can we find the pattern?* Have children look at the row and identify the pattern. Then have them trace or write the missing numbers.

R 6·5

Problem Solving:
Look for a Pattern

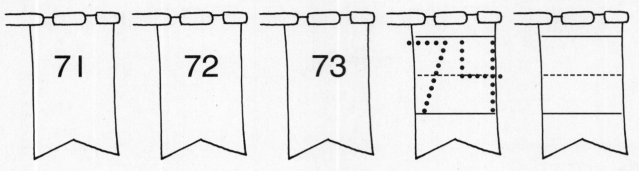

71 72 73 7̣4̣ _____

30 40 50 _____ _____

60 70 80 _____ _____

Directions In each exercise have children identify the number pattern and then continue the pattern by writing the missing numbers.

P 6·5

Stories About Joining

1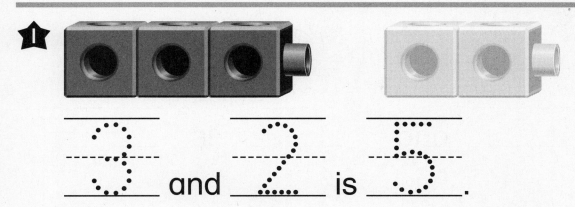

_ _3_ _ and _ _2_ _ is _ _5_ _ .

2

_ _2_ _ and _ _4_ _ is _____ .

3

_____ _____ _____

_____ and _____ is _____ .

Directions Have children: **1** — **2** use cubes to show each story and then trace the number sentence that tells the story. *Ryan has 3 cubes. Then he takes 2 more cubes. How many cubes are there in all? Alica has 2 cubes. Then she takes 4 more. How many cubes are there in all?* **3** *create a story about cubes, draw the cubes, and write the number sentence that tells the story.*

Name _____

Stories About Joining

_____   _____   _____

- - - - - - -   - - - - - - -   - - - - - -

_____ and _____ is _____.

_____   _____   _____

- - - - - - -   - - - - - - -   - - - - - -

_____ and _____ is _____.

_____   _____   _____

- - - - - - -   - - - - - - -   - - - - - -

_____ and _____ is _____.

_____   _____   _____

- - - - - - -   - - - - - - -   - - - - - -

_____ and _____ is _____.

Directions Have children listen to each number story. Then write a number sentence that tells the story. 1 *Rebecca finds 1 red marble. Then she finds 3 blue marbles. How many marbles are there in all?* 2 *Billy picks up 4 pinecones. Then he picks up 2 more. How many pinecones are there in all?* 3 *Rob saw 3 brown leaves. Then he saw 3 yellow leaves. How many leaves are there in all?* 4 *Jill found 3 small bells. Then she found 2 large bells. How many bells are there in all?*

Name _____

More Joining

1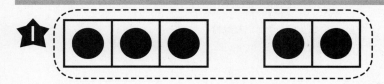

_3_ and _2_ is _5_.

2

_4_ and _____ is _____.

3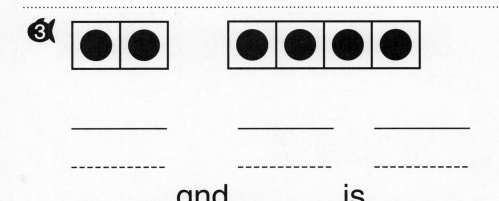

_____ and _____ is _____.

Directions Have children use counters to show each group as you tell a number story. Then have them trace or write numbers to record the number story and circle the counters to find how many in all. ⭐ *Reese shows 3 counters. He shows 2 more counters. How many counters does he show in all?* ❷ *Alisha shows 4 counters. She shows 1 more counter. How many does she show in all?* ❸ *Claire shows 2 counters. She shows 4 more counters. How many counters does she show in all?*

More Joining

1

_____   _____   _____

- - - - -   - - - - -   - - - - -
_____ and _____ is _____ .

2

_____   _____   _____

- - - - -   - - - - -   - - - - -
_____ and _____ is _____ .

3

_____   _____   _____

- - - - -   - - - - -   - - - - -
_____ and _____ is _____ .

4

_____   _____   _____

- - - - -   - - - - -   - - - - -
_____ and _____ is _____ .

Directions Have children write a number for each group. Then have them draw a circle to join the groups and write how many there are in all.

Joining Groups

①

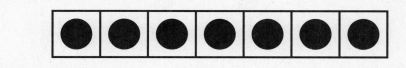

②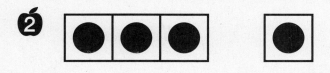

③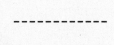

Directions Have children use counters to show each group and then join them. Then have them trace or write the number that tells how many counters there are in all.

Name _____

Joining Groups

_____

- - - - - - - - - -

_____

_____

- - - - - - - - - -

_____

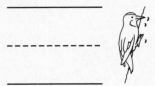

_____

- - - - - - - - - -

_____

_____

- - - - - - - - - -

_____

_____

- - - - - - - - - -

_____

Directions Have children use cubes to show each group and then join the cubes. Then have them write the number that tells how many birds there are in all.

Name _____

Using the Plus Sign

⭐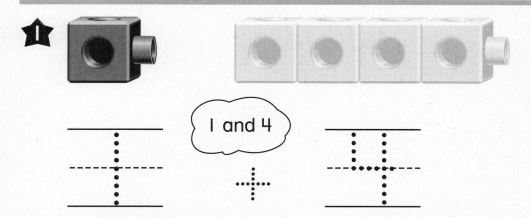

I and 4

❷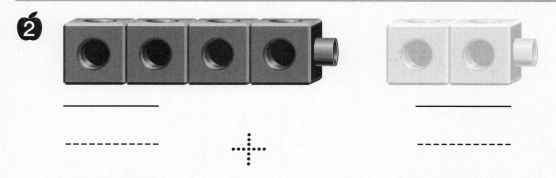

❸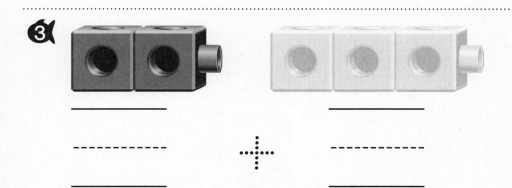

❹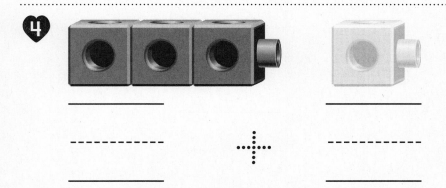

Directions Have children look at the cubes. Then have them trace or write the numbers and a plus sign to show joining the groups of cubes.

R 7·4

Name _____

Using the Plus Sign

5   and   1

____

- - - - - - - - ◯

____   ____

- - - - - - - -

____

2

2   and   3

____

- - - - - - - - ◯   - - - - - - - -

____   ____

3

1   and   2

____   ____

- - - - - - - - ◯   - - - - - - - -

____   ____

Directions Have children look at each picture. Then have them write numbers and a plus sign to show joining the groups.

Name _____

Finding Sums

1   and   4   is   5.

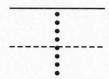 + 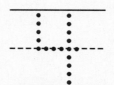 =

3   and   3   is   6.

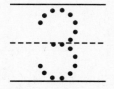 + 3 = _____

5   and   4   is   9.

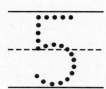 + 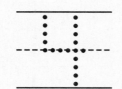 = _____

Directions Have children trace the numbers to tell how many there are in each group. Have them circle the two groups to join them. Then have them trace the plus sign *and* equal sign, and write the sum.

R 7·5

Name _____

Finding Sums

1

$$5 + 5 = 10$$

5   and   5   is   10.

2

$$4 + 2 = 6$$

4   and   2   is   6.

3

$$3 + 6 = 9$$

3   and   6   is   9.

4

$$6 + 1 = 7$$

6   and   1   is   7.

Directions Have children trace the numbers to tell how many there are in each group. Have them circle the two groups to join them. Then have them trace the plus sign and equal sign and write the sum.

Name _____

Addition Sentences

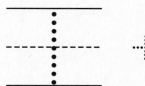 + 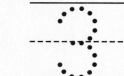 =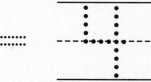

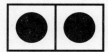

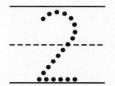 + 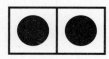 = _____

 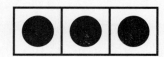

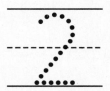 +   = _____

Directions Have children trace the numbers to tell how many there are in each group, show with counters, and join the groups. Then have them trace the plus sign and equal sign and write the sum.

Name _____

Addition Sentences

1

_____   +   _____   =   _____

2

_____   +   _____   =   _____

3

_____   +   _____   =   _____

4

_____   +   _____   =   _____

5

_____   +   _____   =   _____

Directions Have children write the numbers to tell how many there are in each group. Have them circle the two groups to join them. Then have them trace the plus sign and equals sign and write the sum.

Problem Solving: Draw a Picture

1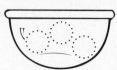

2 + 3 = 5

2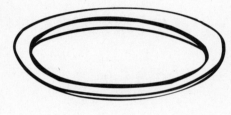

_____ + _____ _:_ _____

3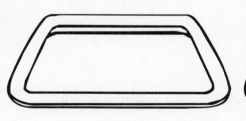

_____ + _____ _:_ _____

Directions *Listen to each story. Draw circles to show the foods. Write the number in each group and the number in all.* **1** *Juanita buys 2 oranges at a fruit stand and 3 more at a supermarket. How many oranges does she buy in all?* **2** *Brian eats 6 crackers. His baby brother eats 2. How many crackers do the boys eat in all?* **3** *There is a plate of 5 red grapes and a plate of 4 green grapes. How many grapes in all?*

Problem Solving: Draw a Picture

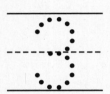 + 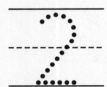 =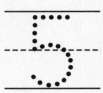

─────
2
───────

─────   ─────   ─────
- - - - -   - - - - -   - - - - -
───── + ───── = ─────

─────
3
───────

─────   ─────   ─────
- - - - -   - - - - -   - - - - -
───── + ───── = ─────

Directions Have children listen to these problems and then draw pictures to solve them. Then have children write the numbers that tell about the picture. ⭐ *Julia has 3 red balls and 2 green balls. How many balls does she have altogether?* ❷ *Luis has 4 yellow balls and 2 red balls. How many balls does he have altogether?* ❸ *Sean has 5 black balls and 1 red ball. How many balls does he have altogether?*

Name _____

Stories About Separating

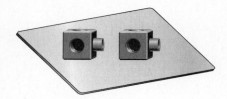 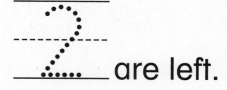

_____
- - - - - -
2 are left.

_____
- - - - - -
3 are left.

_____
- - - - - -
_____ are left.

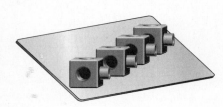

_____
- - - - - -
_____ are left.

Directions Have children listen to number stories and then count how many cubes are left on the mat. Then have them trace or write the number left. ★ *Jessie shows 3 cubes. She takes 1 away. How many cubes are left on the mat?* ② *Alex shows 5 cubes. He takes 2 away. How many cubes are left on the mat?* ③ *Jared shows 8 cubes. He takes 3 away. How many cubes are left on the mat?* ④ Kaitlin shows 5 cubes. She takes 1 away. How many cubes are left on the mat?

Name _____

Stories About Separating

_____

- - - - - - - -

_____ are left.

_____

- - - - - - - -

_____ are left.

_____

- - - - - - - -

_____ are left.

Directions Have children listen to each number story and count how many are left. Then they write the number.
⭐ *Kate sees 6 ducks. 3 ducks fly away. How many ducks are left?* ❷ *Ted sees 6 frogs. 1 frog hops away. How many frogs are left?* ❸ *Lori sees 6 chipmunks. 2 run away. How many are left?*

Stories About Take Away

1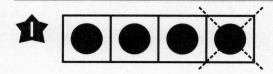

4̲ take away 1 is 3̲.

2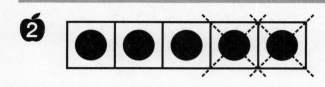

5̲ take away 2 is _____.

3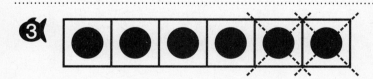

6̲ take away 2 is _____.

Directions Have children listen to each number story and count and trace the number that tells how many in all. Next children trace the Xs to show how many to take away and trace or write the number that tells how many are left. **1** *Jake shows 4 counters. He takes away 1 counter. How many counters are left?* **2** *Katie shows 5 counters. She takes away 2 counters. How many are left?* **3** *Carter shows 6 counters. He takes away 2 counters. How many are left?*

Name _____

Stories About Take Away

1

_____   take away   _____   is   _____ .

2

_____

- - - - - - - - - -   - - - - - - - - - -   - - - - - - - - - -

_____   take away   _____   is   _____ .

3

- - - - - - - - - -

_____   take away   _____   is   _____ .

Directions Have children listen to each number story. Have them count and record the number in all. Ask them to trace or mark Xs to show how many to take away and record this number. Then have children write the number that tells how many are left. **1** *Eric sees 5 geese. Three geese fly away. How many geese are left?* **2** *Eric sees 6 chicks. One chick walks away. How many chicks are left?* **3** *Eric sees 8 ducklings. Three swim away. How many ducklings are left?*

Name _____

Problem Solving: Act It Out

1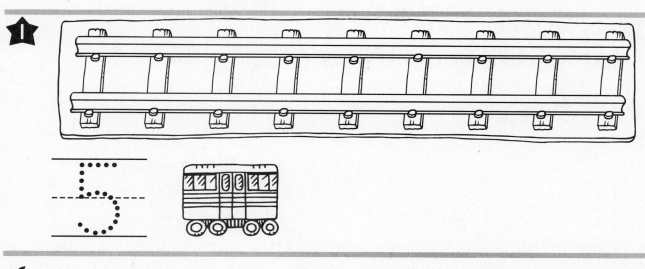

2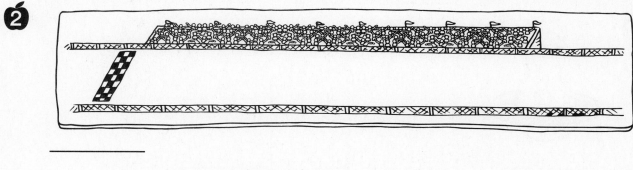

_____
- - - - - - - - -
_____

3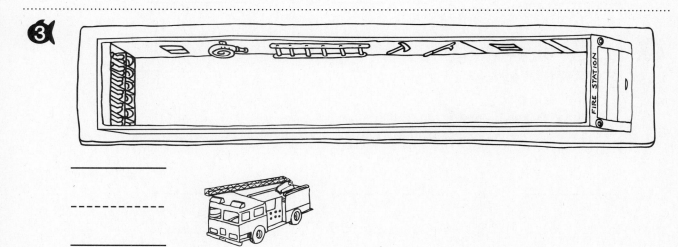

- - - - - - - - -
_____

Directions Have children listen to each problem and solve it by acting it out with cubes. Have them record the answer on the line. **1** *There are 8 train cars on the track. You take 3 cars off the track. How many cars are left on the track?* **2** *There are 7 cars on the track. 4 cars pull off the track. How many cars are left on the track?* **3** *There are 6 fire trucks in the station. 2 trucks leave. How many fire trucks are left in the station?*

Name _____

Problem Solving: Act It Out

1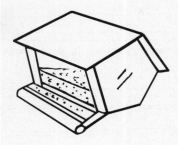

_____   _____   _____

- - - - - - -   - - - - - - - go. - - - - - - -

_____   _____

2

_____   _____

- - - - - - -  - - - - - - - go. - - - - - - -

_____   _____

3

_____   _____

- - - - - - -  - - - - - - - go. - - - - - - -

_____   _____

Directions Have children listen as you tell a problem about each picture. Tell them to solve each problem by acting it out with counters. Have children write each answer.

P 8·3

Using the Minus Sign

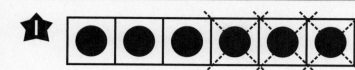

①

②

③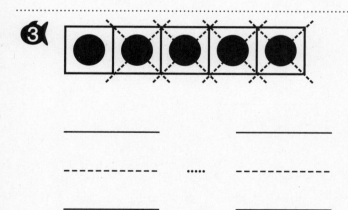

Directions Have children write how many counters there are in all. Have them trace Xs to subtract. Then have them trace the minus sign, write the number subtracted, and tell how many counters are left. Children may use counters to model.

Using the Minus Sign

_____   ......   _____

- - - - - - - - - -   - - - - - - - - - -

_____   _____

❷

_____   _____

- - - - - - - - - -   ......   - - - - - - - - - -

_____   _____

❸

_____   _____

- - - - - - - - - -   ......   - - - - - - - - - -

_____   _____

Directions Have children write how many animals there are in all. Have them trace Xs to subtract. Then have them trace the minus sign, write the number subtracted, and tell how many animals are left.

Finding Differences

1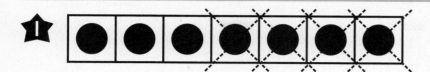

7   take away   4   is   3.

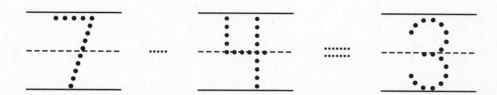

2

6 take away 4   is   2.

_____   _____   _____

3

4 take away 3   is   1.

_____   _____   _____

Directions Have children write how many counters there are in all. Have them trace or mark Xs to subtract. Ask them to trace the minus sign and record the number subtracted. Then have them trace the equal sign and record the difference.

Finding Differences

1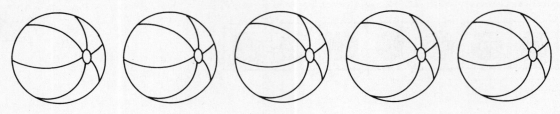

5   take away   2   is   3.

_____   _____   _____
- - - - - - -   .....   - - - - - - -   ::::::   - - - - - - -
_____   _____   _____

2

6   take away   4   is   2.

_____   _____   _____
- - - - - - -   .....   - - - - - - -   ::::::   - - - - - - -
_____   _____   _____

3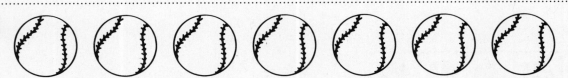

7   take away   1   is   6.

_____   _____   _____
- - - - - - -   .....   - - - - - - -   ::::::   - - - - - - -
_____   _____   _____

Directions Have children write how many balls there are in all. Have them mark Xs to subtract. Ask children to trace the minus sign and write the number subtracted. Then have them trace the equal sign and write the difference.

Name _____

Subtraction Sentences

1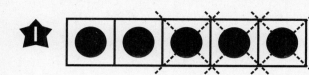

2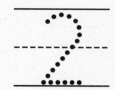

_____   _____   _____

- - - - - - - - -   ·····   - - - - - - - - -   ·······   - - - - - - - - -

_____   _____   _____

3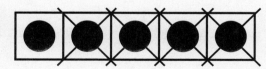

_____   _____   _____

- - - - - - - - -   ·····   - - - - - - - - -   ·······   - - - - - - - - -

_____   _____   _____

Directions Have children record how many counters there are in all. Have them trace or mark Xs to subtract. Ask them to trace the minus sign and record the number subtracted. Then have children complete the subtraction sentence by tracing the equal sign and recording the difference. They may use counters.

Name _____

Subtraction Sentences

_____   _____   _____

- - - - - - - - -   · · · · ·   - - - - - - - - -   ::::::   - - - - - - - - -

_____   _____   _____

_____   _____   _____

- - - - - - - - -   · · · · ·   - - - - - - - - -   ::::::   - - - - - - - - -

_____   _____   _____

 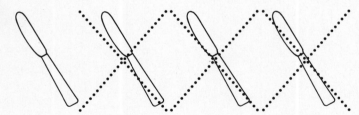

_____   _____   _____

- - - - - - - - -   · · · · ·   - - - - - - - - -   ::::::   - - - - - - - - -

_____   _____   _____

Directions Have children write how many utensils there are in all. Have them trace Xs to subtract. Ask them to trace the minus sign and write the number subtracted. Then have children complete the subtraction sentence by tracing the equal sign and writing the difference.

Subtraction Stories

 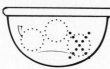

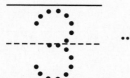 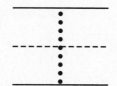 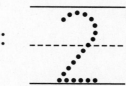

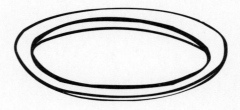

_____ _____ _____ _____ _____

_____   _____

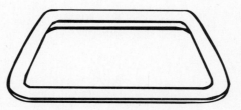

_____ _____ _____ _____ _____

_____   _____

Directions Listen to each story. Draw circles to show the foods and draw Xs to show subtraction. Write the number sentence to match the story and find the difference. ⭐ *Juanita buys 3 oranges and her daughter eats 1 of them. How many oranges does Juanita have left?* 🍎 *Brian has 6 crackers. His baby brother eats 2. How many crackers are left?* 🐟 *There is a plate of 5 red grapes and 4 grapes roll onto the floor. How many grapes are left?*

Subtraction Stories

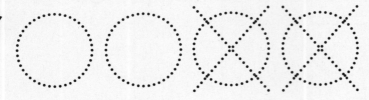

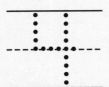 −  =

_____
- - - - -
_____   −   _____   =   _____
- - - - -   - - - - -   - - - - -
_____   _____   _____

_____
- - - - -
_____   −   _____   =   _____
- - - - -   - - - - -   - - - - -
_____   _____   _____

Directions Have children listen to these problems and then draw pictures to solve them. Then have children write the numbers that tell about the picture. ❶ *Julia has 4 red balls and gives 2 away. How many balls does she have left?* ❷ *Luis has 5 yellow balls and gives 1 away. How many balls does he have left?* ❸ *Sean has 5 black balls and gives 3 away. How many balls does he have left?*

Problem Solving: Use Objects

1

5 ○ 2 = 3

2

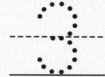

2 ○ ___ = ___

3

6 ○ ___ = ___

Directions Have children listen to each story and use counters to help them solve the problem. If it is a subtraction story, have them trace Xs on the objects that are subtracted. For addition stories, have children draw more objects. Then have them write the addition or subtraction sentence. **1** *Stewart built 5 sandcastles. Waves knocked down 2 of them. How many sandcastles are left?* **2** *Shana saw 2 balls at the beach. Later that day, she saw 3 more balls. How many balls did she see in all?* **3** *Kate baked 6 muffins. Her brother ate 3 of them. How many muffins are left?*

Problem Solving: Use Objects

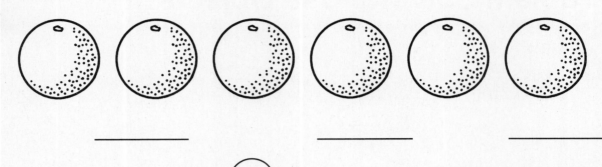

_____   _____
- - - - - - - - -   ◯   - - - - - - - - -   :::::::   - - - - - - - -
_____   _____

2

_____   _____
- - - - - - - - -   ◯   - - - - - - - - -   :::::::   - - - - - - - -
_____   _____

3

_____   _____
- - - - - - - - -   ◯   - - - - - - - - -   :::::::   - - - - - - - -
_____   _____

Directions Have children listen to each story and use counters to help them solve the problem. If it is a subtraction story, have them mark Xs on the objects that are subtracted. Then have them write the addition or subtraction sentence. **1** *Chris picked 6 oranges. He ate 2 of them. How many oranges does Chris have left?* **2** *There are 2 turtles in the pond. 3 more turtles swim over to join them. How many turtles are there in all?* **3** *Catelyn counted 7 butterflies. 5 butterflies flew away. How many butterflies are left?*

P 8·8

Making 4 and 5

1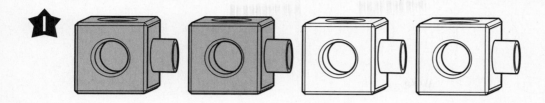

2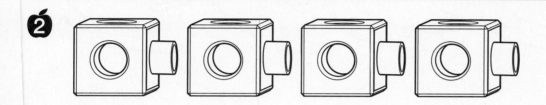

3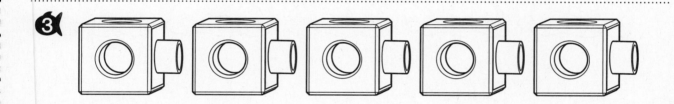

4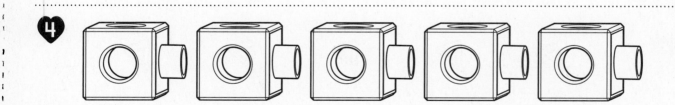

Directions Have children: **1** use red and blue cubes to find one way to make 4 then color the cubes to match; **2** use cubes to find another way to make 4 then color the cubes to match; **3** use red and blue cubes to find one way to make 5 then color the cubes to match; **4** use cubes to find another way to make 5 then color the cubes to match.

R 9·1

Making 4 and 5

 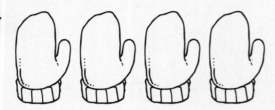

Directions Have children: **1**–**2** color the objects with red and yellow crayons to show different ways to make 4; **3**–**5** color the objects with red and yellow crayons to show different ways to make 5.

Writing Number Sentences
for 4 and 5

1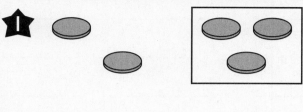

$$5 = 2 + 3$$

2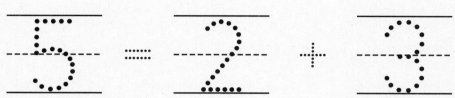

$$\text{---} = \text{---} + \text{---}$$

3

$$\text{---} = \text{---} + \text{---}$$

Directions Have children: **1** count the total number of counters and the number of counters in each set. Then trace the numbers and symbols to write the number sentence. **2**-**3** count the total number of counters and then the parts that are inside and outside the box. Write a number sentence that describes the relationship between the whole and the parts.

Writing Number Sentences
for 4 and 5

 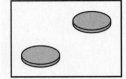

_____ _____ _____

-------- = -------- + --------

_____ _____ _____

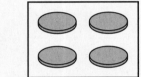

_____ _____ _____

-------- = -------- + --------

_____ _____ _____

_____ _____ _____

-------- = -------- + --------

_____ _____ _____

Directions Have children count the total number of counters, and then the parts that are inside and outside the box. Ask them to write a number sentence that describes the relationship between the whole and the parts.

Name _____

Making 6 and 7

1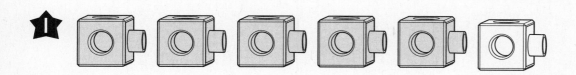

2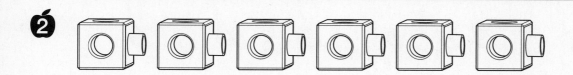

3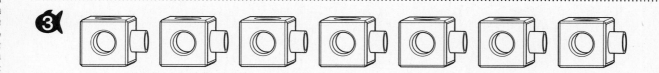

4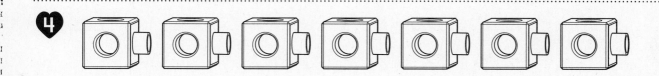

Directions Have children: **1** use red and blue cubes to model the example of one way to make 6; **2** use cubes to find another way to make 6 and then color the cubes to show this way; **3** use red and blue cubes to find one way to make 7 and then color the cubes to show this way; **4** use cubes to find another way to make 7 and then color the cubes to show this way.

Name _____

Making 6 and 7

1

2

3

4

5

Directions Have children: **1**–**3** color the clothes with red and yellow crayons to show different ways to make 6; **4**–**5** color the clothes with red and yellow crayons to show different ways to make 7.

P 9-3

Writing Number Sentences
for 6 and 7

 1

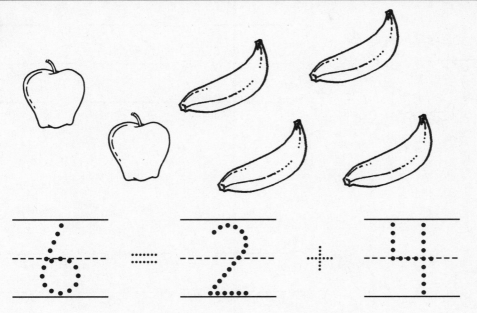

6 = 2 + 4

2

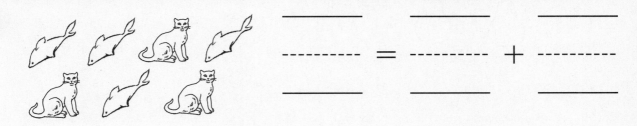

___ ___ ___
----- = ----- + -----
___ ___ ___

3

___ ___ ___
--------- = -------- + --------
___ ___ ___

Directions Have children: 1 count and trace the number sentence that describes the relationship between the total number of items and the parts of the total; 2 - 3 write the number sentence that describes each picture.

R 9·4

Writing Number Sentences
for 6 and 7

⭐**1**

_____ _____ _____

-------- = -------- + --------

_____ _____ _____

🍎**2**

_____ _____ _____

-------- = -------- + --------

_____ _____ _____

3

_____ _____ _____

-------- = -------- + --------

_____ _____ _____

Directions Have children write the number sentence that describes each picture.

Making 8 and 9

1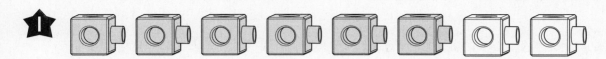

2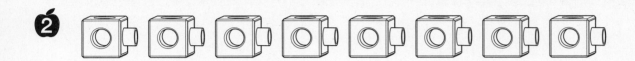

3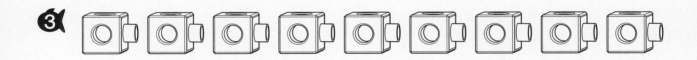

4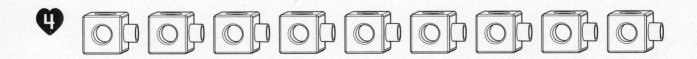

Directions Have children: **1** use red and blue cubes to model the example of one way to make 8 and then color the cubes to match. **2** use cubes to find another way to make 8 and then color the cubes to match; **3** use red and blue cubes to find one way to make 9 and then color the cubes to match; **4** use cubes to find another way to make 9 and then color the cubes to match.

Name _____

Making 8 and 9

1

2

3

4

5

Directions Have children: **1**–**2** color the objects with red and yellow crayons to show different ways to make 8; **3**–**5** color the objects with red and yellow crayons to show different ways to make 9.

Writing Number Sentences
for 8 and 9

1

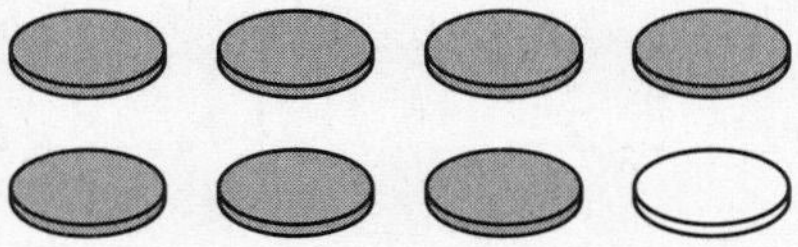

$$8 = 7 + 1$$

In all

$$8 = 1 + 7$$

In all

2

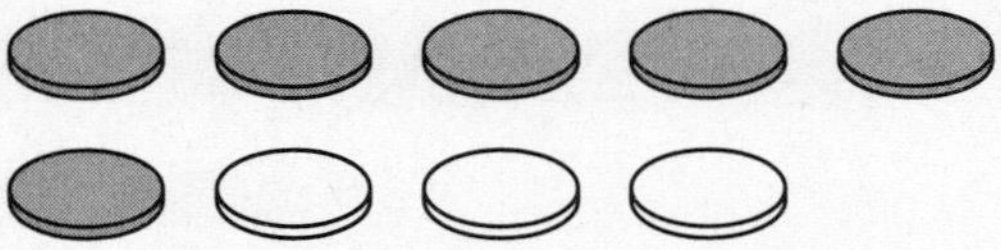

$$\_\_\_ = \_\_\_ + \_\_\_$$

In all

$$\_\_\_ = \_\_\_ + \_\_\_$$

In all

Directions Have children write two different number sentences that describe the picture.

Name _____

Writing Number Sentences
for 8 and 9

1

_____ = _____ + _____

_____ = _____ + _____

2

_____ = _____ + _____

_____ = _____ + _____

3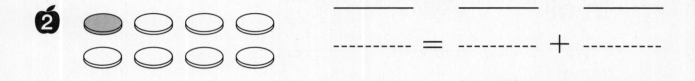

_____ = _____ + _____

_____ = _____ + _____

4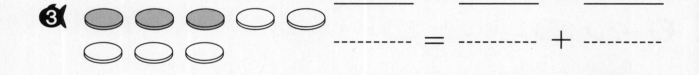

_____ = _____ + _____

_____ = _____ + _____

Directions Have children write two different number sentences to describe the picture.

Name _____

Making 10

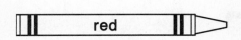 red

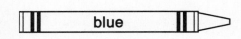 blue

1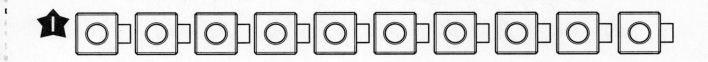

2

3

4

5

Directions In each exercise, have children use red and blue cubes to show different ways to make 10. Then have them use red and blue crayons to record the ways to make 10.

R 9·7

Making 10

1

2

3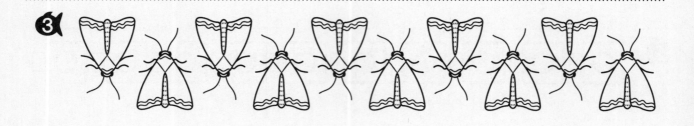

4

5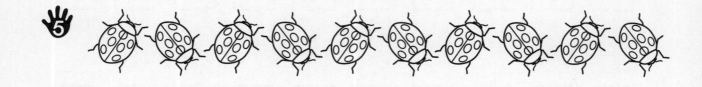

Directions Have children color each picture red or yellow to show different ways to make 10.

Name _____

Writing Number Sentences
for 10

⭐ 10 = 8 + 2

In all

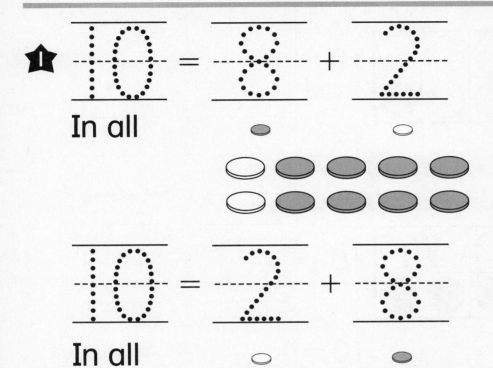

10 = 2 + 8

In all

❷ _____ = _____ + _____

In all

_____ = _____ + _____

In all

Directions Have children write two different number sentences that describe the picture.

Name _____

Writing Number Sentences for 10

 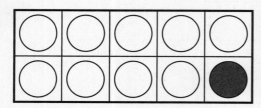

$10 =$ _____ $+$ _____

$10 =$ _____ $+$ _____

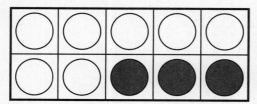

$10 =$ _____ $+$ _____

$10 =$ _____ $+$ _____

3 $\quad 10 = 2 +$ _____

4 $\quad 10 =$ _____ $+ 5$

5 $\quad 10 = 4 +$ _____

Directions Have students: **1** and **2** write two number sentences that describe the picture; **3** – **5** find the missing part and complete the number sentence.

Problem Solving: Make a Graph

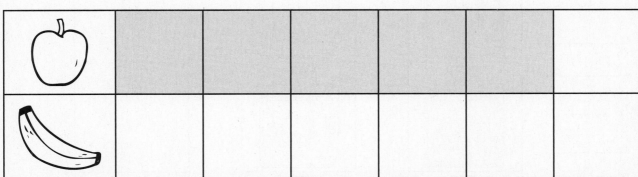

Directions Have children count how many apples there are and shade that many boxes on the graph. Then have children do the same for the bananas. Then have children circle the fruit that has more.

Problem Solving: Make a Graph

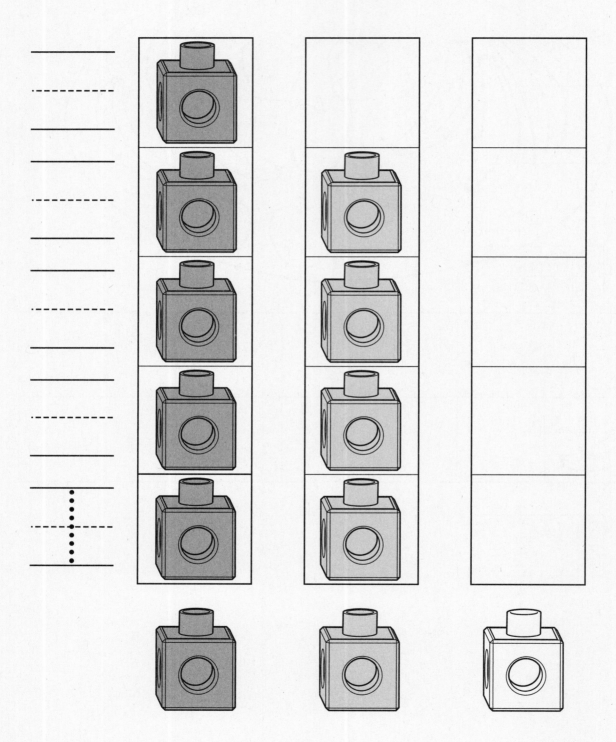

Directions In column 3, have children use cubes to show a group with the fewest cubes. Then have children draw pictures of the cubes in the squares. To complete the graph, have children write the numbers 1–5 up the left side.

Making 11, 12, and 13

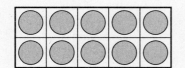 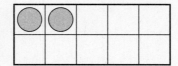

_____ + 2 = 12

1

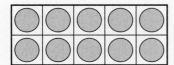 

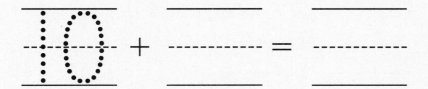

10 + _____ = _____

2

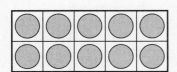 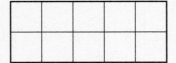

_____ + _____ = _____

Directions Have children complete the drawings and number sentences to make 11 and then 13.

R 10·1

Making 11, 12, and 13

 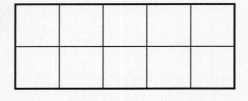 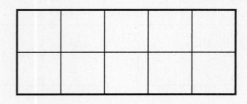

_____   _____   _____

------------ **+** ------------ **=** ------------

_____   _____   _____

 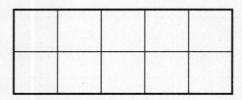

_____   _____   _____

------------ **+** ------------ **=** ------------

_____   _____   _____

❸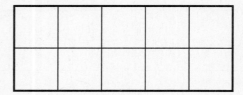

_____   _____   _____

------------ **+** ------------ **=** ------------

_____   _____   _____

Directions Have children: ⭐ write the number sentence and fill in the drawing to show how to make 11; ❷ write the number sentence and fill in the drawing to show how to make 13; ❸ write the number sentence and fill in the drawing to show how to make 12.

Making 14, 15, and 16

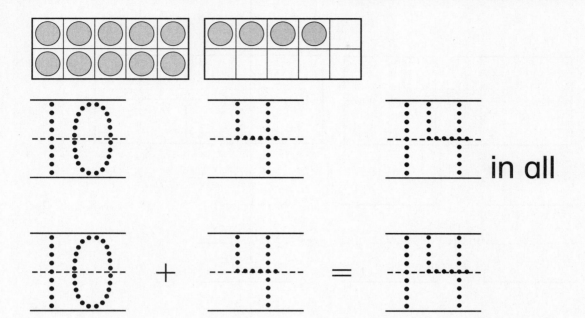

 1

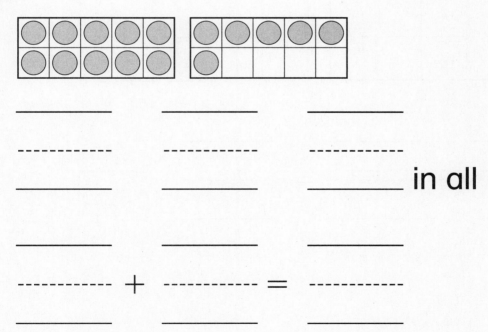

_____ in all

Directions Have children tell how many are in each ten-frame, then tell how many in all, and finally write the number sentence that goes with the picture.

Making 14, 15, and 16

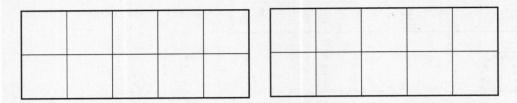

_____   _____   _____

----------- + ----------- = -----------

_____   _____   _____

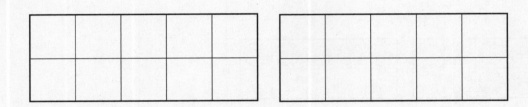

_____   _____   _____

----------- + ----------- = -----------

_____   _____   _____

Directions Have children: ① write the number sentence and fill in the drawing to show how to make 14; ② write the number sentence and fill in the drawing to show how to make 16.

Making 17, 18, and 19

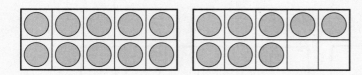

10   8   **18** in all

10 + 8 = 18

★ **1**

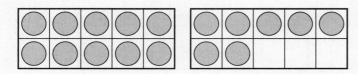

_____ _____   **17** in all

_____ _____ _____

_____ + _____ = _____

_____ _____ _____

Directions Have children tell how many are in each ten-frame, then tell how many in all, and finally write the number sentence that goes with the picture.

Name _____

Making 17, 18, and 19

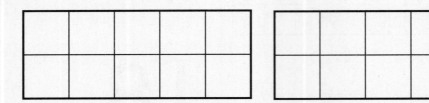

_____   _____   _____

- - - - - - - - - - **+** - - - - - - - - - - **=** - - - - - - - - - -

_____   _____   _____

- -

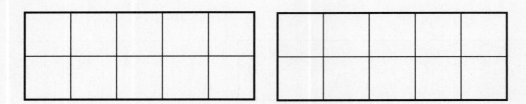

_____   _____   _____

- - - - - - - - - - **+** - - - - - - - - - - **=** - - - - - - - - - -

_____   _____   _____

Directions Have children: ★ write the number sentence and fill in the drawing to show how to make 19; 🍎 write the number sentence and fill in the drawing to show how to make 17.

Problem Solving: Look for a Pattern

| 1 | 2 | 3 | 4 | 5 | **6** | 7 | 8 | 9 | 10 |
| 11 | 12 | 13 | 14 | 15 | **?** | 17 | 18 | 19 | 20 |

_16_ is 10 more than 6.   10 + _6_ = _16_

| 1 | 2 | **3** | 4 | 5 | 6 | 7 | 8 | 9 | 10 |
| 11 | 12 | **?** | 14 | 15 | 16 | 17 | 18 | 19 | 20 |

_____ is 10 more than 3.   10 + _____ = _____

Directions Have children find the missing number in the second row of the hundred chart and complete the sentence and number sentence to show the relationship between the two outlined numbers.

Problem Solving: Look for a Pattern

| 1 | | | | 5 | | | 8 | 9 | |
| 11 | 12 | 13 | | | 16 | | | | 20 |

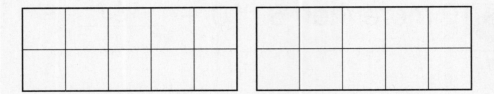

_____   _____   _____

---------- + ---------- = ------------

_____   _____   _____

Directions Have children: ⭐ complete the first two rows of the hundred chart; 🍎 fill in the ten frames to show the number in the heavily outlined box, and then write a number sentence to match the ten frames.

P 10·4

Name ______________________

Reteaching
11-1

Creating Sets to 19

1

10 and 9 is 19.

2

10 and 7 is ______.

3

10 and ______ is ______.

Directions Have children complete the number sentences to show how many counters there are in the double ten-frames.

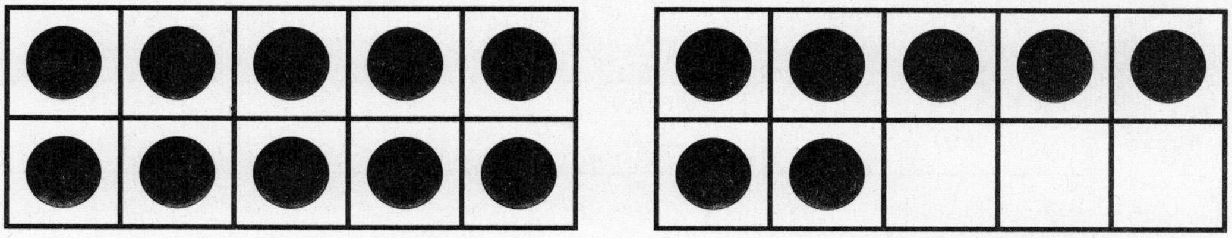

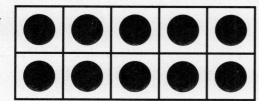

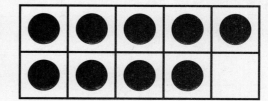

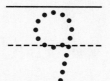

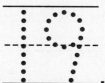

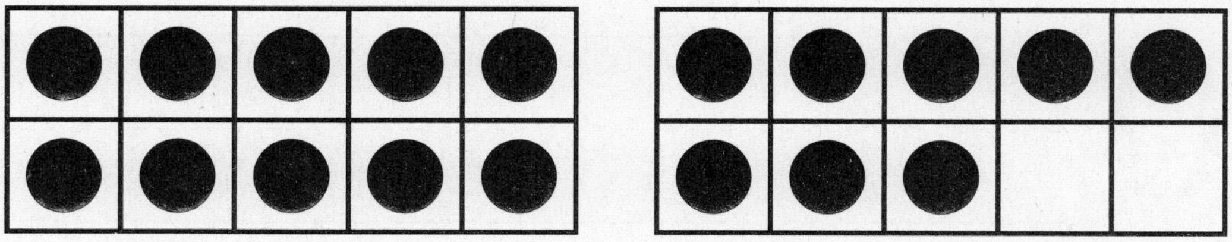

Creating Sets to 19

★ 10 _____
_____

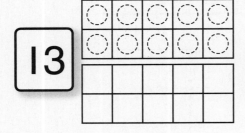

13   10 and _____ is _____.

❷ 10 _____
_____

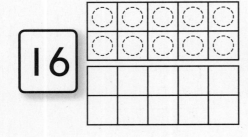

16   10 and _____ is _____.

❸ 10 _____
_____

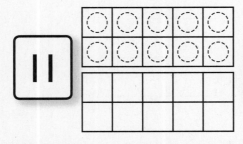

11   10 and _____ is _____.

Directions Have children draw counters in the double ten-frame to show the number on each number card. Then have them show the number by counting on from 10 and then by adding a number to 10.

Name _____

Parts of 11, 12, and 13

 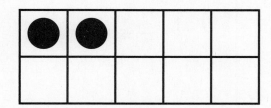

$12 = 10 + 2$

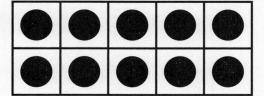

$11 = 10 + \underline{\hspace{1cm}}$

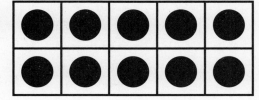

$13 = \underline{\hspace{1cm}} + \underline{\hspace{1cm}}$

Directions Have children look at the groups of ten-frames and complete the number sentences.

Parts of 11, 12, and 13

 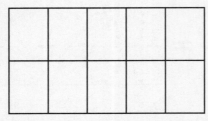

$$11 = 10 + \underline{\hspace{2cm}}$$

$$12 = 10 + \underline{\hspace{2cm}}$$

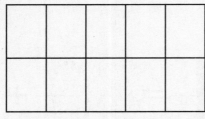

$$13 = 10 + \underline{\hspace{2cm}}$$

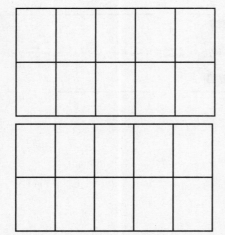

Directions Have children: ★ color boxes in the ten-frames to show 11 and write the missing number; ❷ color boxes in the ten-frames to show 12 and write the missing number; ❸ color boxes in the ten-frames to show 13 and write the missing number.

Parts of 14, 15, and 16

 1

| 15 |

15 = 10 + 5

2

| 16 |

16 = 10 + _____

3

| 14 |

14 = _____ + _____

Directions Have children trace or draw counters in the double ten-frame to show the number on the number card. Then have them complete each number sentence.

Parts of 14, 15, and 16

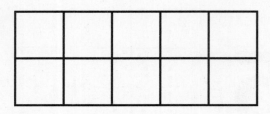 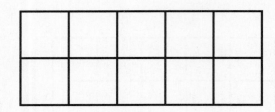

_____ _____   _____

---------- = ---------- + ----------

_____ _____   _____

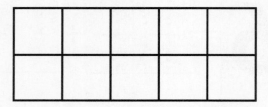 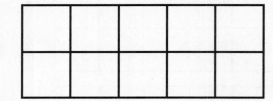

_____ _____   _____

---------- = ---------- + ----------

_____ _____   _____

Directions Have children: ★ draw counters in the ten-frames to show 14 as one ten and some more ones and then write a number sentence that describes the drawing; 🍎 draw counters in the ten-frames to show 15 as one ten and some more ones and then write a number sentence that describes the drawing.

Parts of 17, 18, and 19

1

17

17 = 10 + 7

2

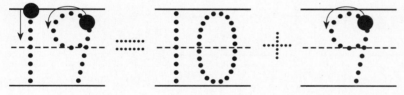

19 = 10 + 9

3

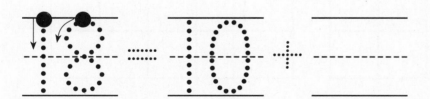

18 = 10 + ____

Directions Have children: **1** count the counters in the ten-frames and trace the number sentence to match the ten-frames; **2** count the counters in the ten-frames and trace the number sentence to match the ten-frames; **3** count the cubes in the cube train and complete the number sentence to match the cube train.

R 11·4

Name _____

Parts of 17, 18, and 19

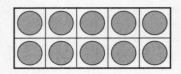 

_____   _____   _____

- - - - - - - - - - = - - - - - - - - - - + - - - - - - - - - -

_____   _____   _____

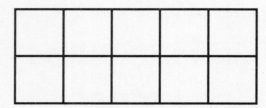

2

_____   _____   _____

- - - - - - - - - - = - - - - - - - - - - + - - - - - - - - - -

_____   _____   _____

3 17 = 10 + 7

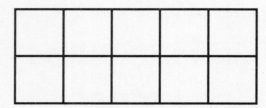   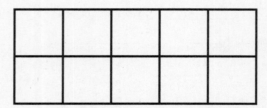

Directions Have children: ⭐ count the counters in the ten-frames and write a number sentence to match the ten-frames; 🍎 count the cubes in the cube train and write a number sentence to match the cube train; ✖ color the ten-frames to match the number sentence.

Problem Solving: Look
for a Pattern

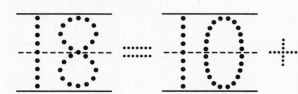

18 = 10 + 8

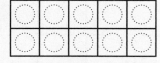

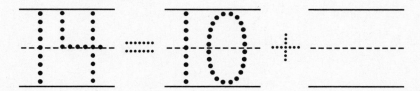

14 = 10 + _____

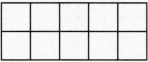

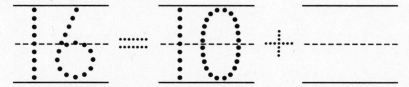

16 = 10 + _____

Directions Have children: ① trace 18 counters in the ten-frames and complete the number sentence; ② trace 14 counters in the ten-frames and complete the number sentence; ③ draw the counters in the second ten-frame to show 16 and complete the number sentence.

Problem Solving: Look
for a Pattern

 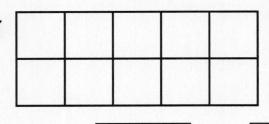 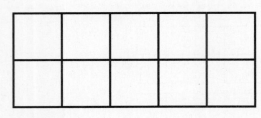

15 = _____ + _____

2

19 = _____ + _____

3

_____

_____ = _____ + _____

Directions Have children: **1** draw 15 counters as one ten, or ten ones, and some additional ones and then complete the number sentence; **2** draw 19 counters as one ten, or ten ones, and some additional ones and then complete the number sentence; **3** look at the counters and write a number sentence to match the picture.

Describing Objects by More Than One Attribute

1

2

3

Directions Have children look at each object, describe the attributes of the object, and circle the tools that they can use to tell about the attributes of the object.

Name _____

Describing Objects by More Than One Attribute

Directions Have children look at each object, describe the attributes of the object, and circle the tools they could use to tell about the attributes of the object.

Comparing by Length

1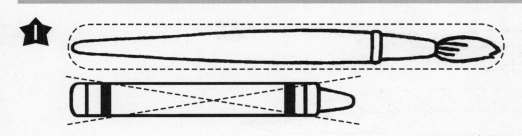

2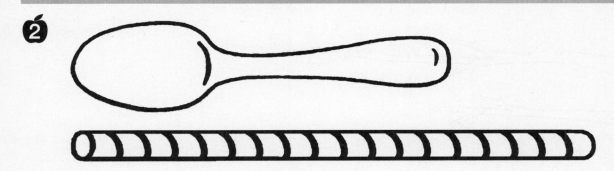

3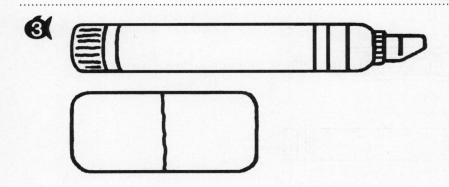

4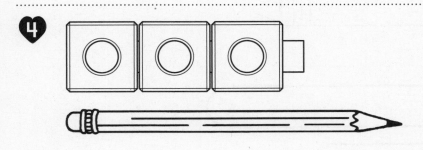

5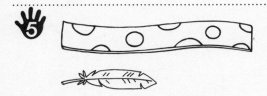

Directions Have children: **1** circle the longer object and mark an X on the shorter object; **2**–**3** circle the longer object; **4**–**5** mark an X on the shorter object.

Comparing by Length

1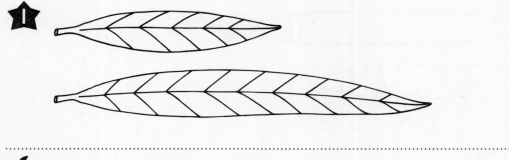

2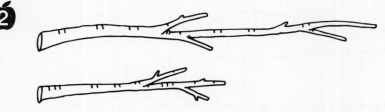

3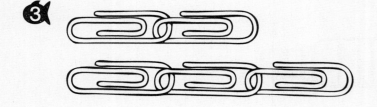

4

5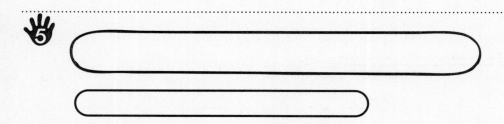

Directions Have children circle the longer object and mark an X on the shorter object. If the objects are the same length, underline both of them.

More Comparing Objects by Length

①

②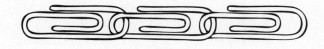

③

Directions Have children color the longest object red and the shortest object yellow.

Name _____

More Comparing Objects by Length

1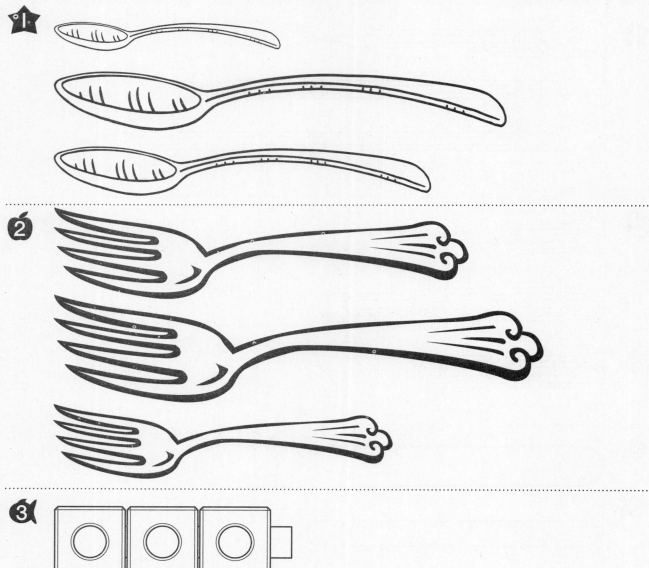

2

3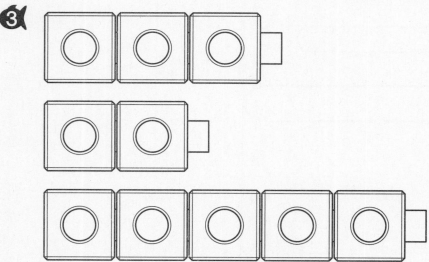

Directions Have children circle the longest object and mark an X on the shortest object.

Problem Solving:
Try, Check, and Revise

⭐ **1**

🍎 **2**

🐦 **3**

❤️ **4**

Directions *Jared is using paper strips for a project. He tries to order the paper strips from shortest to longest. How can we check his work?* Provide children with paper strips that measure 2 inches, 3 inches, 4 inches, and 5 inches. Have children compare and order the paper strips from shortest to longest and then write the numbers to show the correct order from shortest to longest (1–4).

Name _____

Problem Solving:
Try, Check, and Revise

_____
- - - - - - - - -
_____

_____
- - - - - - - - -
_____

_____
- - - - - - - - -
_____

_____
- - - - - - - - -
_____

Directions *Olivia wants to compare pieces of ribbon to find the shortest and longest. How can we compare the pieces? How can we check and revise?* Have children compare and order the pieces of ribbon from shortest to longest, write the numbers to show the correct order from shortest to longest (1–4), and then discuss the process and results.

Name _____

Comparing by Height

1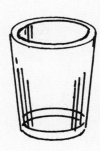

2

3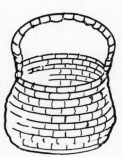

Directions Have children circle the taller object.

Comparing by Height

1

2

3

4

5

6

Directions Have children circle the taller object and mark an X on the shorter object. If the objects are the same height, underline both of them.

Name _____

More Comparing Objects by Height

 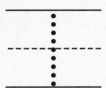 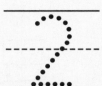 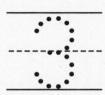

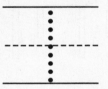 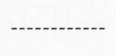 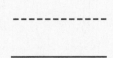

 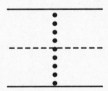 

Directions Have children write the numbers 1, 2, and 3 to show the containers in order from shortest to tallest.

Name _____

More Comparing Objects by Height

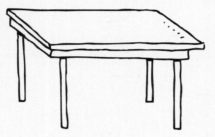  

  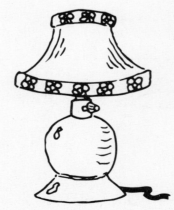

Directions Have children circle the tallest object and mark an X on the shortest object.

Name _____

Comparing Capacities

Directions Have children color the watering can that holds more green and the watering can that holds less yellow. Then have them look at each of the other four pairs of containers, and color the one in each pair green that holds more; color yellow the container in each pair that holds less.

Name _____

Comparing Capacities

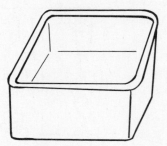

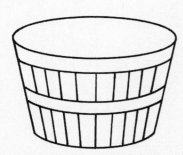

Directions Have children compare objects by drawing a line from the object on the left that holds less to the matching object on the right that holds more.

Comparing by Weight

1
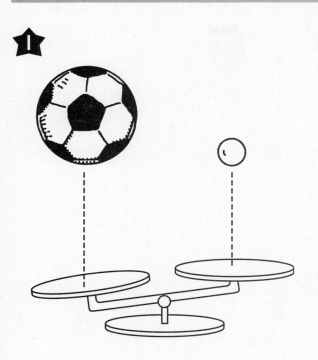

2
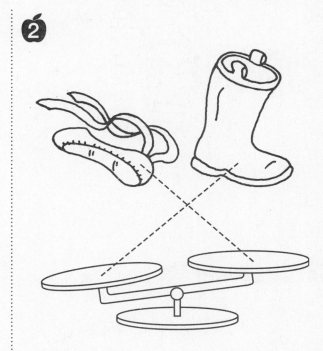

3

4

Directions Have children look at the objects and decide which object is heavier and which object is lighter. Then have them match the heavier object to the low side of the scale and match the lighter object to the high side of the scale.

Name _____

Comparing by Weight

1

2

3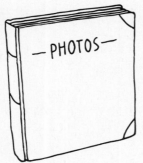

4

5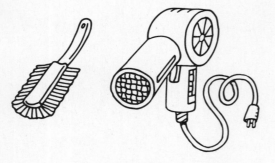

6

Directions Have children compare each pair of objects and then mark an X on the lighter object.

Same and Different

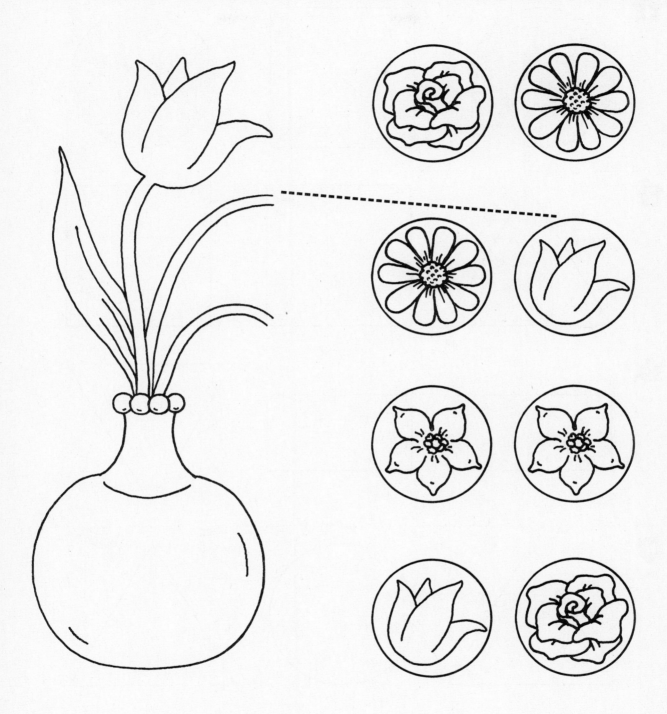

Directions Have children find the flower stickers that are the same as the flower in the vase and draw a line from them to the stems in the vase.

Name _____

Same and Different

  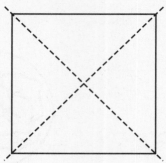 

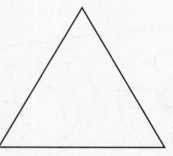  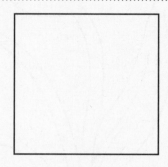

 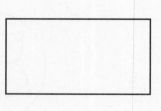 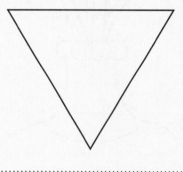

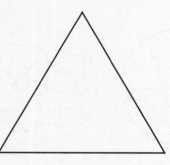 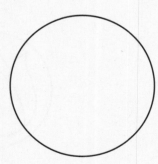 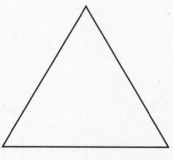

Directions Have children color the same two items in each row the same color. Have them mark an X on the item in each row that is different from the other two items.

Name _____

Sorting by One Attribute

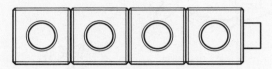

RED

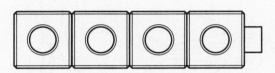

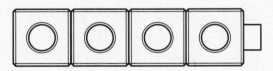

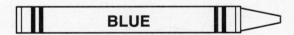
BLUE

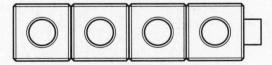

Directions Display a container with 8 red and 8 blue cubes. Have children: ⭐ take a handful of cubes, sort the red cubes by placing 1 on each cube outline, then color the outlines to show their red cubes; 🍎 take another handful, sort the blue cubes, then color to show their blue cubes.

R 13·2

Name _____

Sorting by One Attribute

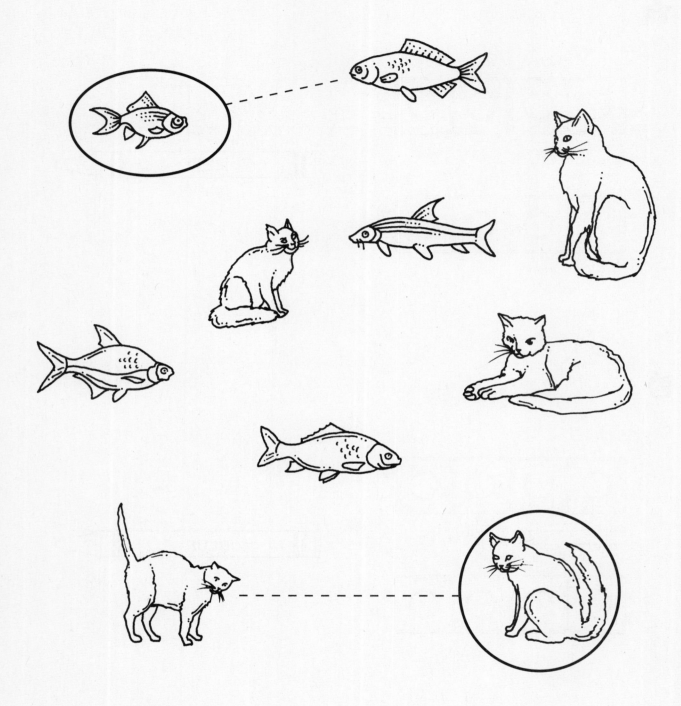

Directions Have children sort the cats and the fish by drawing lines to the appropriate circles.

Sorting the Same Set in Different Ways

1

2

Directions Have children: **1** sort the presents one way and circle the presents to show how they sorted; **2** sort the same presents a different way and circle to show how they sorted.

R 13·3

Name _____

Sorting the Same Set in Different Ways

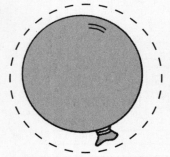   

Directions Have children: ⭐ sort the balloons by circling all the large balloons; 🍎 sort the balloons by circling all the shaded balloons.

Name _____

Sorting by More Than One Attribute

 1

2

Directions Have children: **1** sort the shapes one way by drawing them in the space provided; **2** sort the shapes a different way by drawing them. Then ask children to explain how they sorted each set, by shape, design, or size.

R 13·4   Copyright © Pearson Education, Inc., or its affiliates. All Rights Reserved. K

Name _____

Sorting By More Than One Attribute

1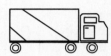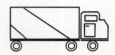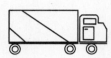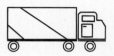

2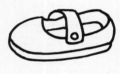

3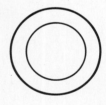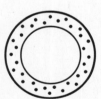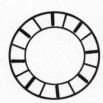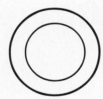

4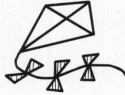

Directions Have children look at the objects in each row and mark an X on the object that doesn't belong.

Problem Solving: Use Logical Reasoning

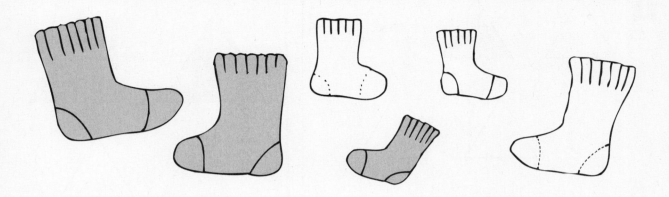

1

2

Directions Have children: **1** use yellow and red crayons to draw the socks and sort them by color; **2** draw socks to sort them by size.

Name _____

Problem Solving: Use Logical Reasoning

1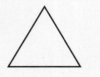

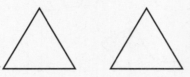

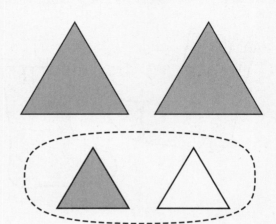

2

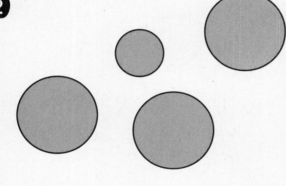

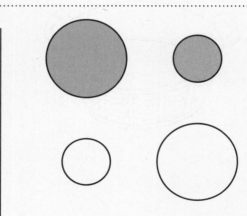

3

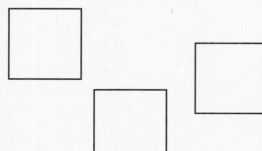

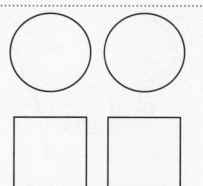

Directions For each exercise, have children identify how the attribute blocks are sorted on the left and circle the blocks on the right that show the sorting rule.

Name _____

Real Graphs

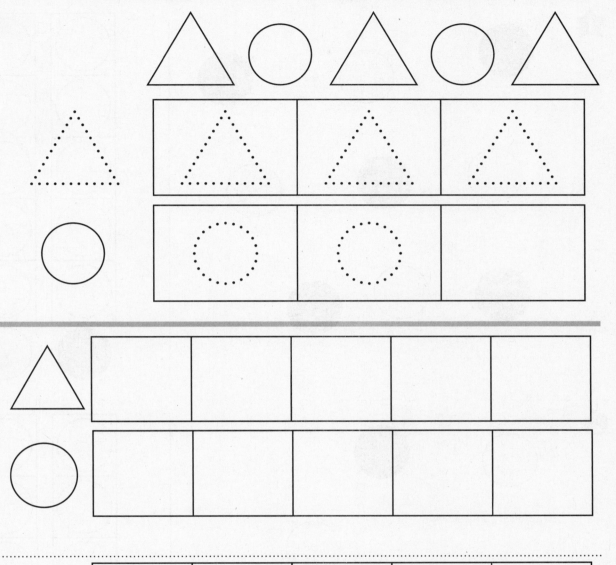

Directions Children will need the attribute blocks shown for these exercises. Have children: sort the blocks by shape, trace each shape, count how many of each shape there are, and circle the row with the most shapes; ❷–❸ take a handful of triangle and circle blocks, sort and count them by shape, and draw how many of each type they pick up each time in the graphs.

R 13·6

Real Graphs

       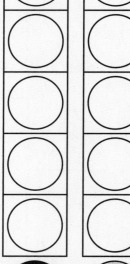

Directions Have children: ★—❷ count how many counters of each color there are, and color to show the number of each color counter in the graphs on the right. Then, circle the column that shows which group has fewer objects.

Picture Graphs

 1

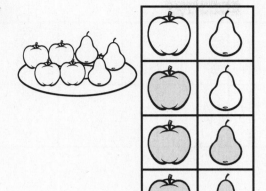

 **2**

3

4

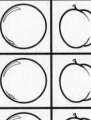
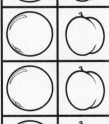

Directions Have children look at the fruit on each plate and color a picture on the graph for each one. Then have children count how many are in each column, and circle the fruit at the bottom of the column that shows more.

R 13·7

Name _____

Picture Graphs

1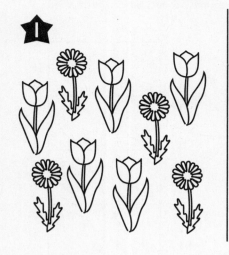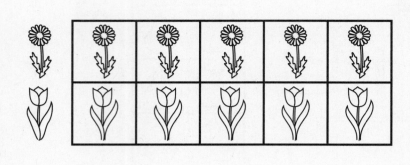

2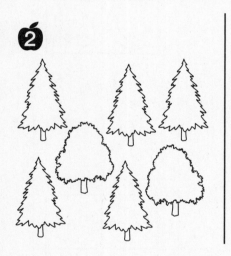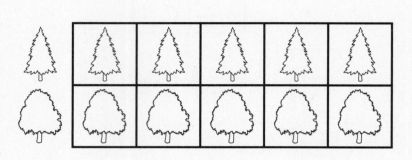

3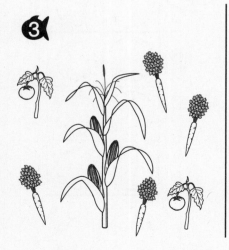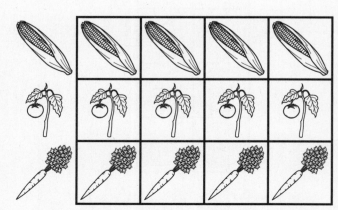

Directions Have children count how many of each object there are, and color a picture on the graph for each object. Then have them circle the row in each graph that has more or the most objects.

Rectangles

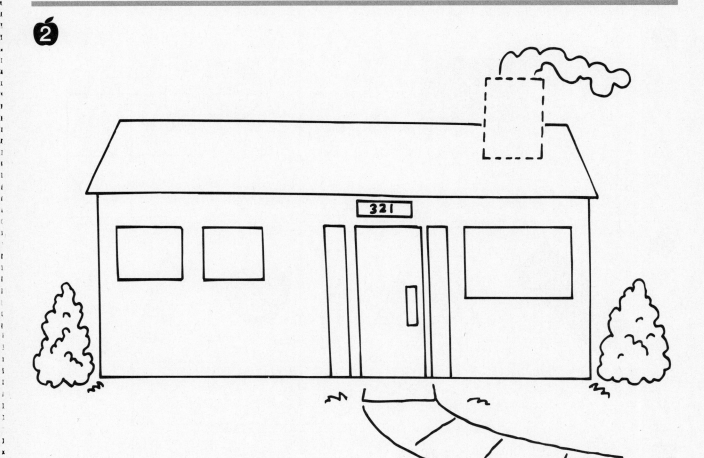

Directions Have children: ⬆ describe the rectangle street sign and trace the shape next to it to complete the rectangle sign; ❷ trace the rectangle to make a chimney and then trace the other rectangles in the picture.

R 14·1   Copyright © Pearson Education, Inc., or its affiliates. All Rights Reserved. **K**

Name _____

Rectangles

  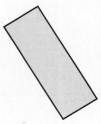

 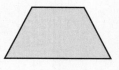   

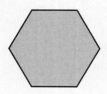   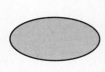

Directions Have children circle the rectangles.

Squares

1

 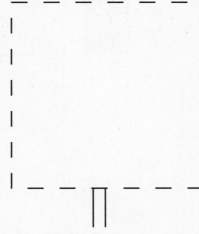 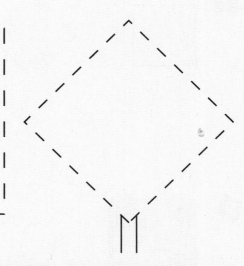

2

SCHOOL

Directions Have children: **1** describe the square sign and trace the shapes next to it to complete the square signs; **2** circle the signs that are shaped like a square.

Name _____

Squares

1

2

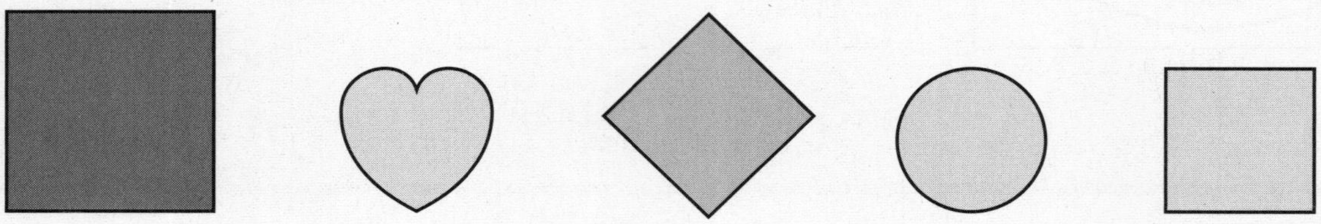

3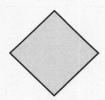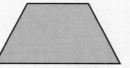

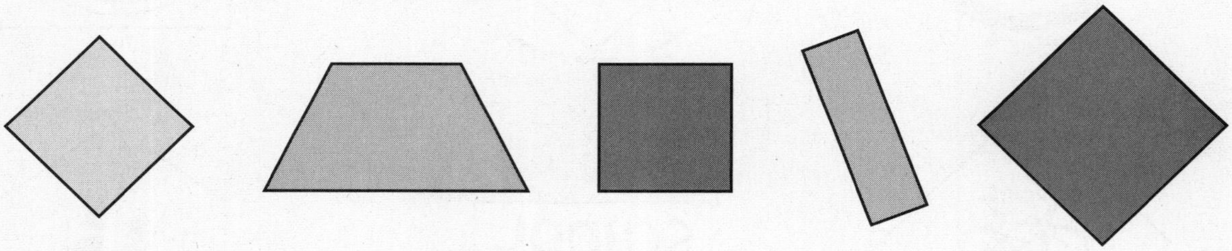

4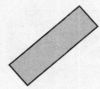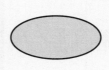

Directions Have children circle the squares.

Name _____

Circles

Directions Have children: explain how a circle is different than a square and trace the circles; ❷ color the objects that are shaped like a circle.

Name _____

Circles

1

2

3

4

Directions Have children mark an X on the circles.

Triangles

 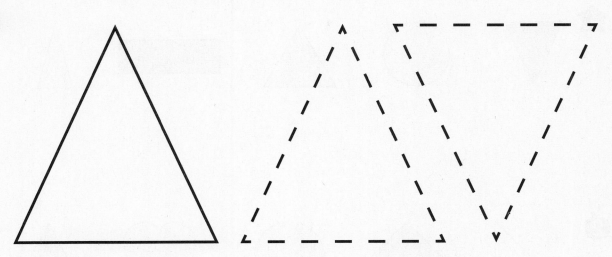

Directions Have children: explain how a triangle is different than a square and trace the triangles; color the blocks that are shaped like a triangle.

Name _____

Triangles

1

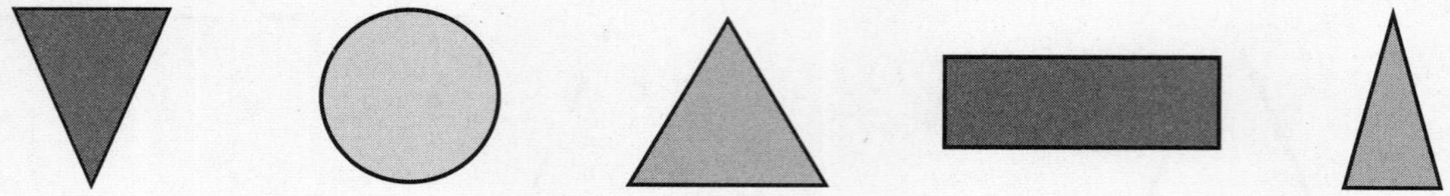

2

3

4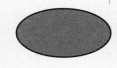

Directions Have children circle the triangles.

Hexagons

1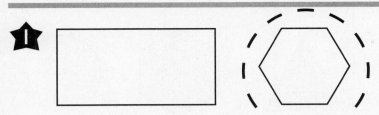

2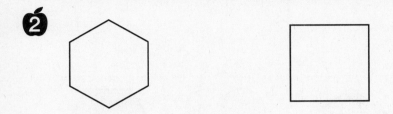

3

4

5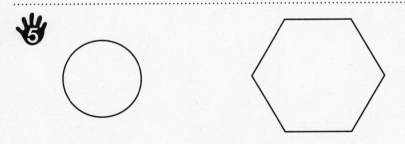

6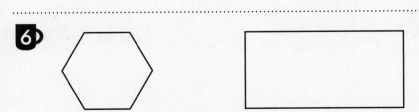

Directions Have children circle the hexagon.

R 14·5

Name _____

Hexagons

1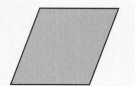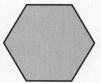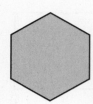

2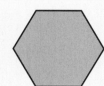

3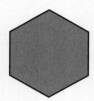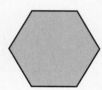

4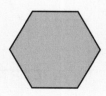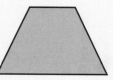

Directions Have children circle the hexagons.

Solid Figures

 1

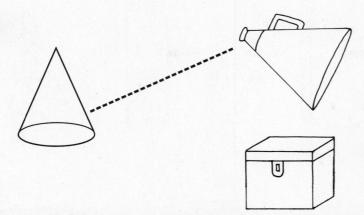

2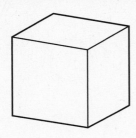

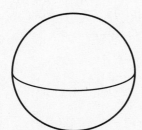   

Directions Have children draw a line from the solid figure to the object that has the same shape.

Name _____

Solid Figures

1 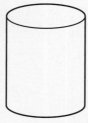   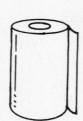

2 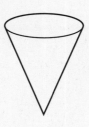   

3 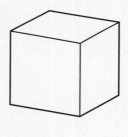   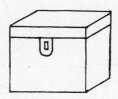

4 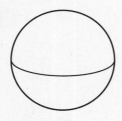   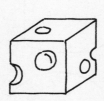

Directions Have children name the solid figure on the left and then circle the objects on the right that have the same shape.

Name _____

Flat Surfaces of Solid Figures

①

②

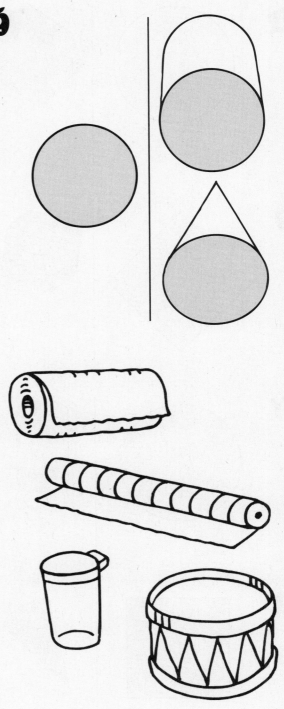

Directions Have children look at the shape at the top and color the same flat surface on the solid figures below.

Name ______________________________

Flat Surfaces of Solid Figures

Practice
14-7

1

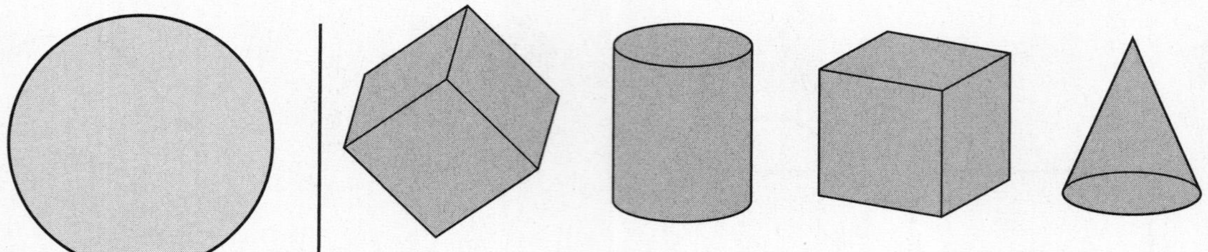

2

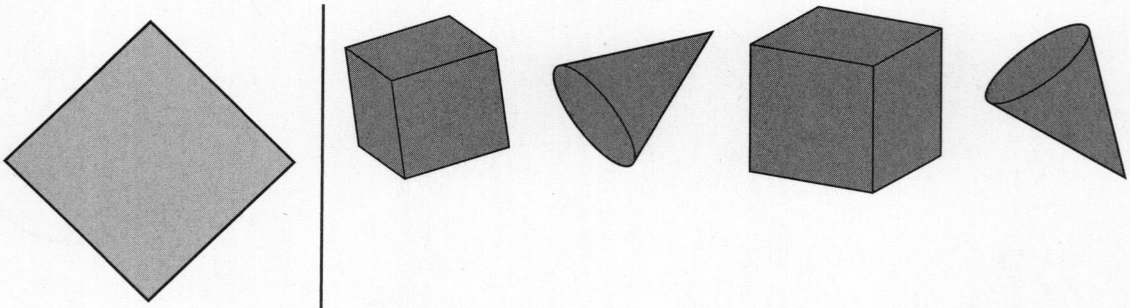

3

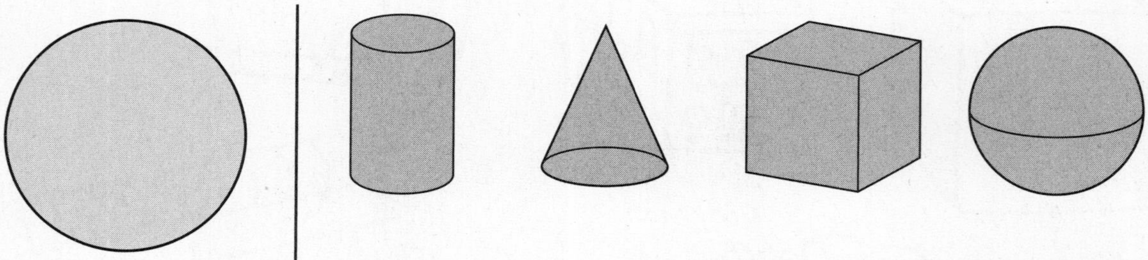

4

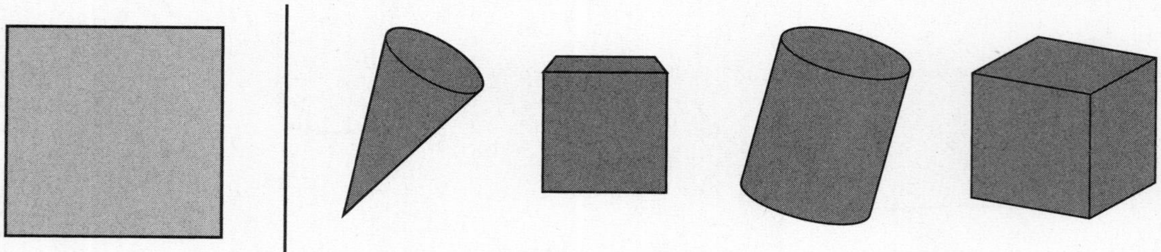

Directions Have children look at the shape on the left. Then have them circle the solid figures that have that flat surface.

Name _____

Problem Solving: Use Objects

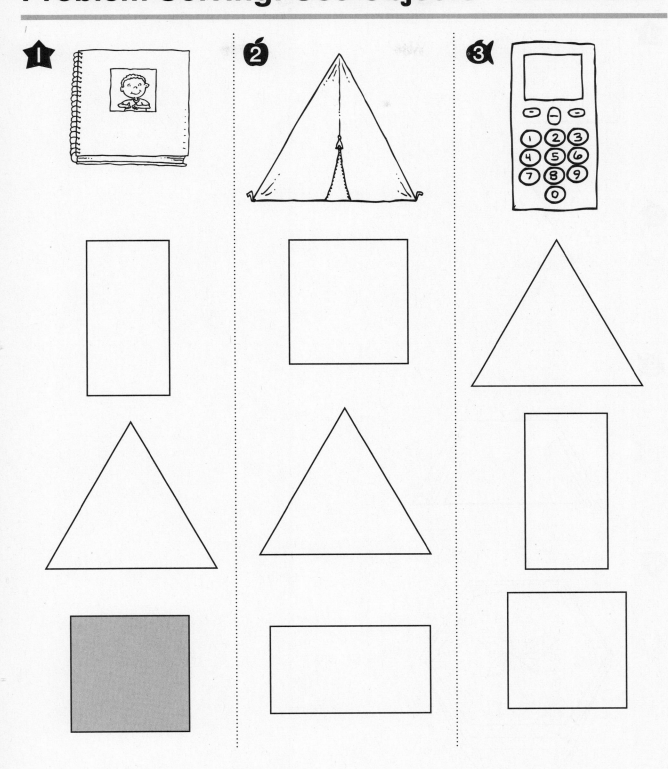

Directions *How can we find the shape of an object? What can we use? How can we check?* Have children use attribute blocks to match the shapes. Then have them color the block that matches the shape of the pictured object.

Problem Solving: Use Objects

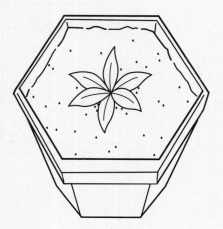

Directions Have children find the pattern block that matches the shape of each pictured object, trace the pattern block, and then explain how they know that the shapes match.

Inside and Outside

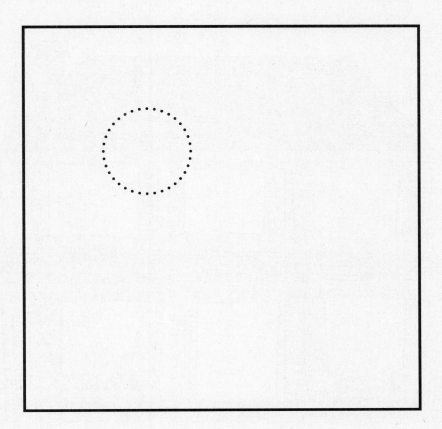

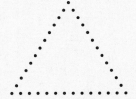

Directions Have children find the circle inside the square and trace it, and then find the triangle outside the square and trace that. Then have them draw more circles inside the square and more triangles outside the square. Have children color a circle inside the square red and a triangle outside the square blue.

R 15·1 Copyright © Pearson Education, Inc., or its affiliates. All Rights Reserved. K

Name _____

Inside and Outside

Directions Have children draw a clock and a picture inside the house. Then have them draw a pail and a drum outside the house.

Above, Below, and On

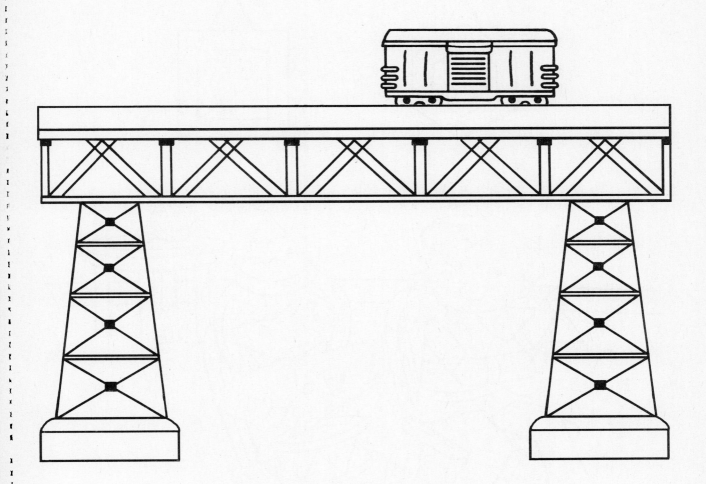

Directions Have children look at the train bridge, point to the train car on the bridge, and then draw rectangles on the bridge. Then have them draw a circle above the bridge and triangles below the bridge.

Name _____

Above, Below, and On

Directions Have children mark an X on the picture above the boy, the hat below the chair, the bird on the boy, and the yarn below the table. Work with children to identify real-world plane and solid shapes in the picture.

Name _____

In Front Of and Behind

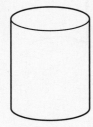  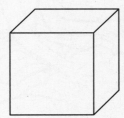 

 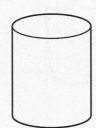  

Directions Have children: ★ draw a square in front of the rabbit; ❷ draw a circle behind the rabbit; ❸ circle the bird next to the cylinder; ❹ circle the bird beside the sphere.

Name _____

In Front Of and Behind; Next To and Beside

Directions Have children: ❶ draw a beach ball in front of the boy; ❷ circle the pail behind the boy; ❸ mark an X on the lunch box in front of the boy; ❹ circle the basket next to, or beside, the boy.

P 15·3

Name _____

Left and Right

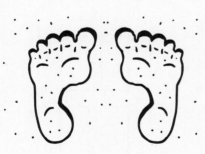

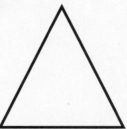

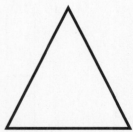

Directions Have children: ❶ circle the water fountain on the left and circle the boy on the right; ❷ circle the hand on the left; ❸ circle the square on the left; ❹ circle the footprint on the right; ❺ circle the triangle on the right.

R 15·4

Name _____

Left and Right

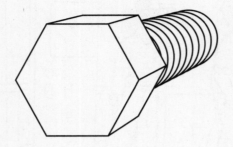 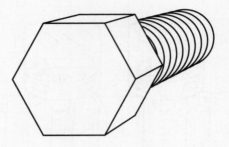

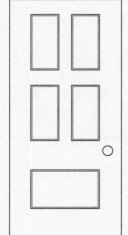 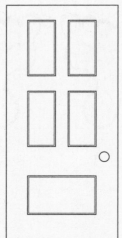

Directions Have children color the bolt on the right blue, the pizza on the left red, the instrument on the right orange, and the door on the left yellow.

Problem Solving: Act It Out

 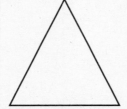 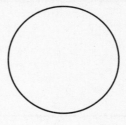 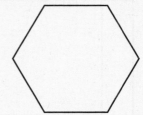

 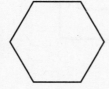

Directions Have children mark the best answer. ⭐ Which picture shows the cow next to the barn? ❷ Which shape is to the right of the circle?

Problem Solving: Act It Out

Directions *Justin wants to draw objects to complete the picture. How can he do that?* Have children: ❶ draw a block below the piggy bank; ❷ draw a ball to the left of the piggy bank; ❸ draw a hat on the doll on the left; ❹ draw a book next to the block.

Creating 2-D Shapes

 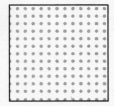

Directions Have children use yarn, pipe cleaners, or straws to make each shape. Children should attach any shape they make with materials to the page.

R 16·1

Name _____

Creating 2-D Shapes

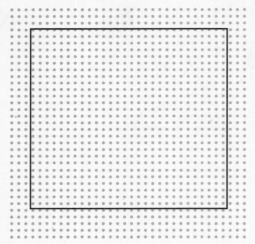

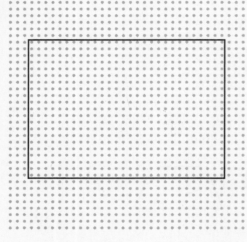

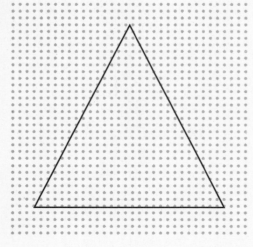

Directions Have children draw or use yarn, pipe cleaners, or straws to make each shape. Children should attach any shape they make with materials to the page.

Name _____

Making Shapes
from Other Shapes

  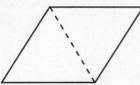   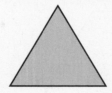   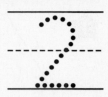

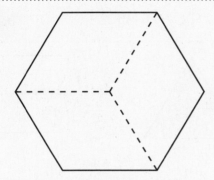   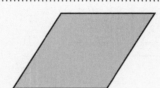   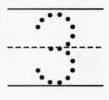

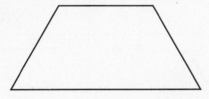   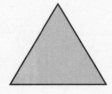

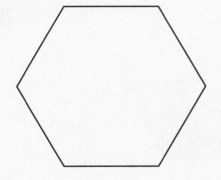   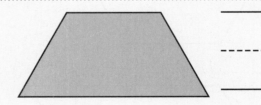

Directions Have children cover the shape on the left with the pattern block shown, draw the lines, and then write the number that tells how many blocks are used.

R 16·2

Name _____

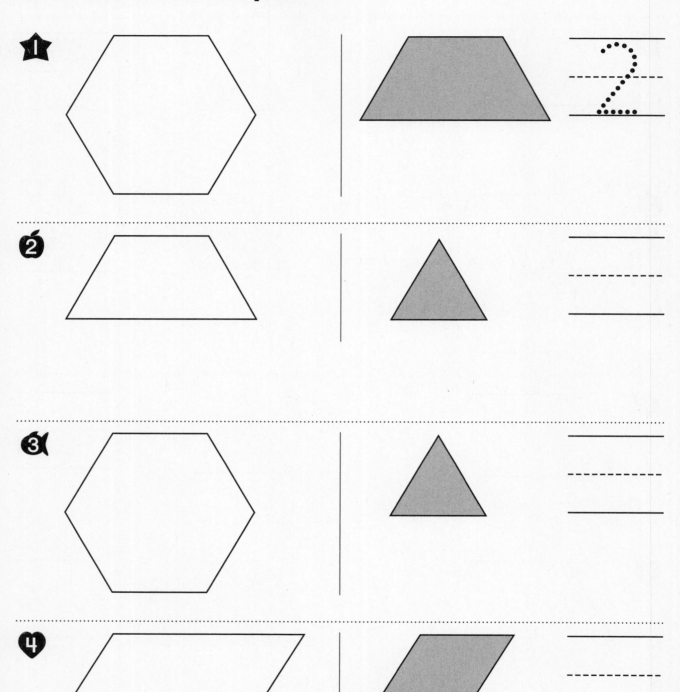

Making Shapes
from Other Shapes

① 2

②

③

④

Directions Have children cover the shape on the left with the pattern block shown, draw the lines, and then write the number that tells how many blocks are used.

Name _____

Comparing Solid Figures

1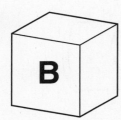

2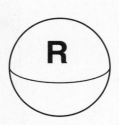

3

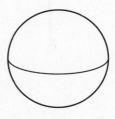

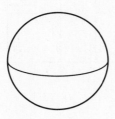

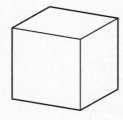

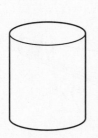

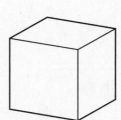

Directions Have children: **1** color the solid figures that can stack on any other figure blue; **2** color the solid figures that can roll red; **3** color the solid figures that can slide green.

Name _____

Comparing Solid Figures

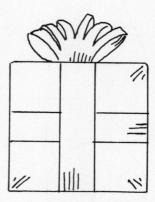

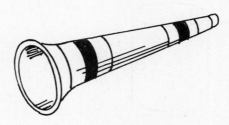

Directions Have children circle all the solid figures that can roll. Then have them mark an X on all the solid figures that can slide. Point out that some objects that are circled should also be marked with an X.

Building with Solid Figures

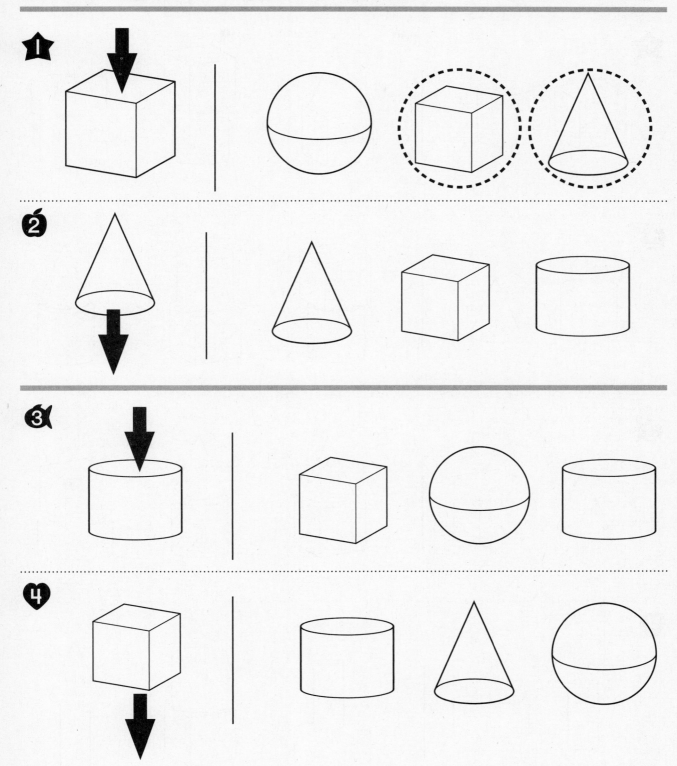

Directions Have children: ❶ circle the solid figures that can be stacked on the cube; ❷ circle the solid figures on which the cone can be stacked; ❸ circle the solid figures that can be stacked on the cylinder; ❹ circle the solid figure on which the cube can be stacked.

Name _____

Building with Solid Figures

1
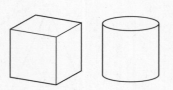 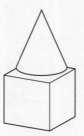 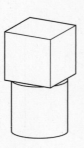 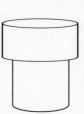

2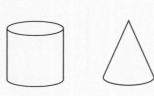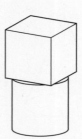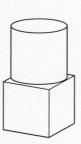

3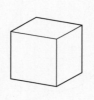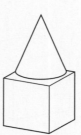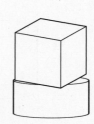

4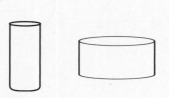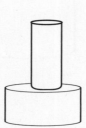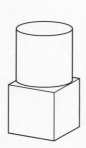

Directions Have children circle the shape that could be made when the 2 solid figures on the left are put together.

Problem Solving:
Use Logical Reasoning

 1

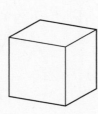 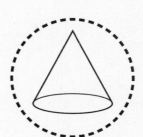

2

3

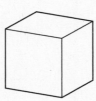

4

Directions Read the clues to children. Have them circle the shape that the clues describe. **1** *I can slide and roll. Which shape am I?* **2** *I can roll but* ***cannot*** *stack. Which shape am I?* **3** *I can stack and slide. Which shape am I?* **4** *I have only 1 flat surface. Which shape am I?*

Problem Solving:
Use Logical Reasoning

 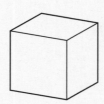

 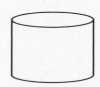

  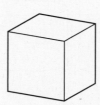

Directions Have children mark an X on the shapes that do **not** fit the clues and circle the shape that the clues describe. **1** *I can roll and slide. I have only 1 flat surface.* **2** *I can roll. I have no flat surfaces.* **3** *I can roll, stack, and slide. I have 2 flat surfaces.* **4** *All of my flat surfaces are squares.*

Introducing Addition Number Sentences

Join the parts to make the whole.

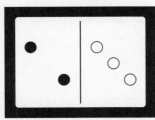

How many black counters?

How many white counters?

__2__ and __3__ is __5__ in all. 5 is the sum of 2 and 3.

Add to find the sum. Use counters if you like.

1.

How many black counters? _____

How many white counters? _____

__4__ and __2__ is __6__ in all. 6 is the sum of 4 and 2.

2.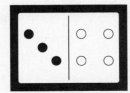

_____ and _____ is _____ in all.

3.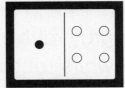

_____ and _____ is _____ in all.

4.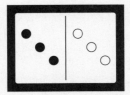

_____ and _____ is _____ in all.

5.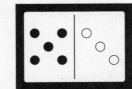

_____ and _____ is _____ in all.

Introducing Addition Number Sentences

Use the picture. Write an addition sentence.

1.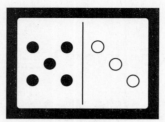

_____ + _____ = _____

2.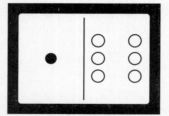

_____ + _____ = _____

Visual Thinking

3. Which addition sentence goes with the question?

There are 3 gray rabbits in the garden.
There are 4 white rabbits.
How many rabbits are there in all?

Ⓐ $3 + 4 = 7$

Ⓑ $4 + 4 = 8$

Ⓒ $3 + 6 = 9$

Ⓓ $3 + 1 = 4$

Name _____

Stories About Joining

Join the groups to find how many bugs in all.

Use a counter for each bug. Then count.

2 bugs are on the rock.

2 bugs are on the blanket.

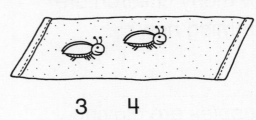

1   2

3   4

How many bugs are there in all?   4   bugs

Tell a joining story for each picture.
Use counters to tell how many in all.

1. 1 bird is in a tree.

2 birds are in a nest.

How many birds are there in all?   _____ birds

2. 3 fish are in a bowl.

2 fish are in another bowl.

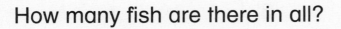

How many fish are there in all?   _____ fish

Stories About Joining

Write an addition sentence. Solve.

1. 4 children are swimming.
   Then 4 more children join them.

   How many children are
   swimming now?

   ____ + ____ = ____

2. 6 puppies are playing.
   Then 2 more puppies join them.

   How many puppies
   are playing now?

   ____ + ____ = ____

3. 2 fish are in the tank.
   Then 4 more fish join them.

   How many fish are in the
   tank now?

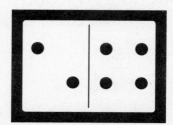

   ____ + ____ = ____

Algebra

4. Which number makes the addition sentence
   true?

   $$4 + \rule{2cm}{0.15mm} = 6$$

   1   2   3   6
   Ⓐ   Ⓑ   Ⓒ   Ⓓ

Adding in Any Order

You can add in any order and get the same sum.

4 + 2 = 6   2 + 4 = 6

Add. Write an addition sentence with
the addends in a different order.

1.

3 + 2 = 5   2 + 3 = 5

2.

___ + ___ = ___   ___ + ___ = ___

3.

___ + ___ = ___   ___ + ___ = ___

4. 2
      +5
      [ ]

   [ ]
  + [ ]
   [ ]

5. 6
      +3
      [ ]

   [ ]
  + [ ]
   [ ]

Adding in Any Order

Write the sum.
Then change the order of the addends.
Write the new addition sentence.

1. 5 + 3 = ___

___ + ___ = ___

2. 4 + 2 = ___

___ + ___ = ___

3. 1 + 3 = ___

___ + ___ = ___

4.

8

+ 1

___

9

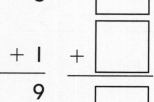

5.

3

+ 4

___

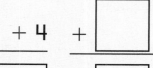

6.

9

+ 0

___

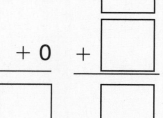

Algebra

7. Which is the same
as 4 + 1?

(A) 1 + 5

(B) 4 + 3

(C) 2 + 5

(D) 1 + 4

8. Which is the same
as 6 + 3?

(A) 3 + 2

(B) 5 + 2

(C) 3 + 6

(D) 7 + 0

Introducing Subtraction Number Sentences

You can write a subtraction sentence to find how many are left.

___4___ take away ___1___ is ___3___.

___4___ minus ___1___ equals ___3___.

4   –   1   =   3

This is a subtraction sentence.

1.

3 minus 1 equals ___2___.

3 – 1 = 2

2.

5 minus 2 equals ___3___.

5 – 2 = 3

Journal

3. Draw a picture that shows subtraction.
Write a subtraction sentence that tells about your picture.

Introducing Subtraction Number Sentences

Write a subtraction sentence.

1.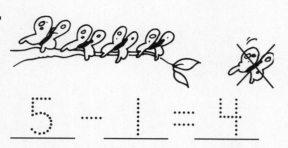

$$5 - 1 = 4$$

2.

___ ..... ___ ..... ___

3.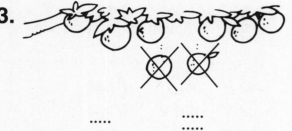

___ ..... ___ ..... ___

4.

___ ..... ___ ..... ___

5.

___ ..... ___ ..... ___

6.

___ ..... ___ ..... ___

Number Sense

7. Draw the missing dots.
Which subtraction sentence
tells about the model?

Ⓐ 8 − 2 = 6   Ⓒ 8 − 4 = 4

Ⓑ 8 − 6 = 2   Ⓓ 4 − 4 = 0

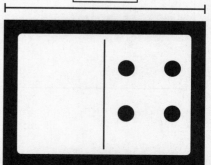

Name _____

Stories About Taking Away

There are 5 birds on the branch.
3 birds fly away.
How many birds are left?

You need to find how many birds are left.
Write a subtraction sentence to find
how many birds are left.

$$\underline{5} - \underline{3} = \underline{2}$$

Check to see if your answer makes sense.

Write a subtraction sentence to answer
each question.

1. There are 7 marbles
   in the bag.
   2 marbles roll out.
   How many marbles
   are left in the bag?

   $$\underline{} - \underline{} = \underline{}$$

2. Jill has 10 pencils.
   She gives 4 pencils to Sam.
   How many pencils does
   Jill have left?

   $$\underline{} - \underline{} = \underline{}$$

Stories About Taking Away

Find the difference. Write a subtraction sentence.

1.

There are 5 children at the table.
2 children stop eating.
How many children are still eating?   ____ − ____ = ____

2.

A man has 6 balloons.
1 balloon flies away.
How many balloons does
the man have now?   ____ − ____ = ____

Algebra

3. 9 children are jumping rope.
3 children leave to play tag.
How many children are still jumping rope?
Which subtraction sentence tells
about the story?

| 9 |

Ⓐ 9 − 1 = 8   Ⓒ 9 − 5 = 4

Ⓑ 9 − 4 = 5   Ⓓ 9 − 3 = 6

Using Fact Families

This is a fact family.

$8 + 3 = 11$

$3 + 8 = 11$

$11 - 8 = 3$

$11 - 3 = 8$

Each number sentence has the same 3 numbers.

Complete each fact family. Use counters to help you.

1. | 6 | 10 | 4 |

$6 + 4 = 10$

$4 + 6 = 10$

$10 - 4 = 6$

$10 - 6 = 4$

2. | 8 | 5 | 13 |

$8 + 5 = \underline{\hspace{1cm}}$

$5 + \underline{\hspace{1cm}} = 13$

$13 - 5 = \underline{\hspace{1cm}}$

$13 - \underline{\hspace{1cm}} = 5$

3. | 7 | 5 | 12 |

$7 + 5 = \underline{\hspace{1cm}}$

$5 + \underline{\hspace{1cm}} = 12$

$12 - 5 = \underline{\hspace{1cm}}$

$12 - \underline{\hspace{1cm}} = 5$

Name _____

Using Fact Families

Write the fact family for the model.

1.

_____ + _____ = _____

_____ + _____ = _____

_____ − _____ = _____

_____ − _____ = _____

2.

_____ + _____ = _____

_____ + _____ = _____

_____ − _____ = _____

_____ − _____ = _____

....

Reasoning

Solve the problem.

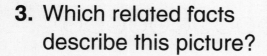

3. Which related facts
describe this picture?

Ⓐ $4 + 11 = 15, 15 − 4 = 11$ Ⓒ $2 + 4 = 6, 4 + 2 = 6$

Ⓑ $10 − 4 = 6, 6 + 4 = 10$ Ⓓ $6 − 4 = 2, 6 − 2 = 4$

Numbers Made with Tens

You can count the models to find out how many groups of ten.

1 ten is 10. 2 tens is 20. 3 tens is 30. 4 tens is 40.

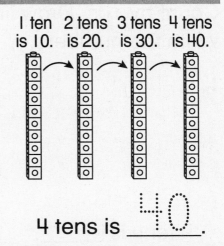

1 ten is 10.
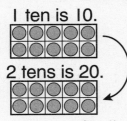
2 tens is 20.

1 ten is 10.
2 tens is 20.
3 tens is 30.

2 tens is __20__. 3 tens is __30__. 4 tens is __40__.

Count the models. Write how many. Then write the number.

1.

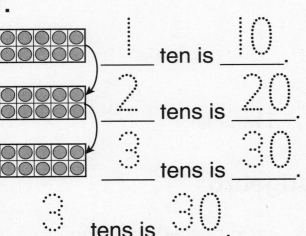

__1__ ten is __10__.

__2__ tens is __20__.

__3__ tens is __30__.

__3__ tens is __30__.

2.

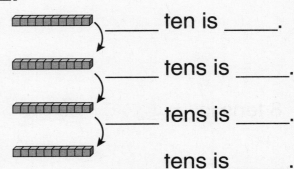

_____ ten is _____.

_____ tens is _____.

_____ tens is _____.

_____ tens is _____.

_____ tens is _____.

3.

_____ ten is _____.

_____ tens is _____.

_____ tens is _____.

_____ tens is _____.

_____ tens is _____.

_____ tens is _____.

Name _____

Numbers Made with Tens

Count by 10s. Draw lines for the cube trains.
Write the numbers.

1.

4 tens is _____.

2.

7 tens is _____.

3.

8 tens is _____.

4.

5 tens is _____.

5. What number is shown?

Ⓐ 2

Ⓑ 10

Ⓒ 12

Ⓓ 20

Algebra

6. Jean has 60 marbles. 40 of the marbles are in one bag. The rest are in another bag. How many marbles are in the second bag?

Ⓐ 40

Ⓑ 30

Ⓒ 20

Ⓓ 10

Counting with Groups of 10 and Leftovers

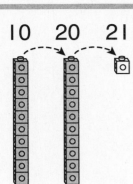

10 20 21

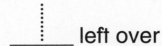

__2__ groups of 10   __1__ left over   __21__ in all

Use counters to show the cubes.
Make groups of 10.
Then write the numbers.

10 11 12 13 14 15 16 17

_____ group of ten

_____ left over

_____ in all

_____ groups of ten

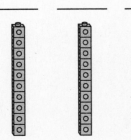

_____ left over

_____ in all

Counting with Groups of 10 and Leftovers

Circle groups of 10.
Write the numbers.

1.

1 group of 10 and 5 left over is _____.

2.

3 groups of 10 and 6 left over is _____.

3. Writing in Math

10 beads fit on a bracelet.
Ben has 54 beads.
Draw a picture to show
all the bracelets he
can make with his beads.
Then draw the beads
that will be left over.

Properties of Plane Shapes

Count the straight sides.	Count the corners.	
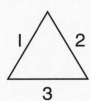	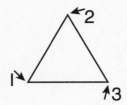	
A triangle has _____ straight sides.	A triangle has _____ corners.	A circle has _____ sides. A circle has _____ corners.

Count the straight sides. Count the corners.

1.

A square has ___4___
straight sides.

A square has ___4___
corners.

2.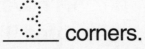

A hexagon has _____
straight sides.

A hexagon has _____
corners.

3. Draw a shape with fewer than 5 corners.

4. Draw a shape with fewer than 5 straight sides.

Name _____

Properties of Plane Shapes

1. Draw a shape with 5 corners.

2. Draw a shape with 4 straight sides.

3. Draw a shape with 3 sides and 3 corners.

4. I have 4 sides and 4 corners. Which shape am I?

Ⓐ circle

Ⓑ trapezoid

Ⓒ hexagon

Ⓓ triangle

Reasoning

Here is the way Brian sorted some plane shapes.

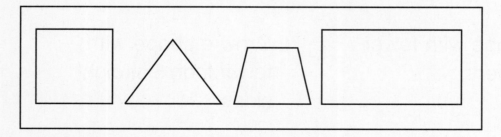

Circle the question Brian might have asked.

Does it have fewer than 5 corners?

Does it have more than 5 straight sides?

Name _____

Flat Surfaces and Vertices

These solid figures have **flat surfaces.**

These solid figures have **vertices** or corners.

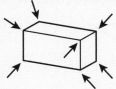

Use solid figures to complete the table.

Solid Figure	Number of Flat Surfaces	Number of Vertices (Corners)
1.	6	8
2.		
3.		
4.		

Flat Surfaces and Vertices

Circle the solid figure that answers each question.

1. Which solid figures have 6 flat surfaces and 8 vertices?

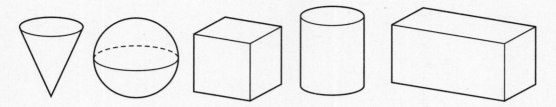

2. Which solid figure has 0 flat surfaces and 0 vertices?

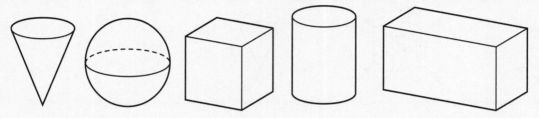

3. Which solid figure has 2 flat surfaces and 0 vertices?

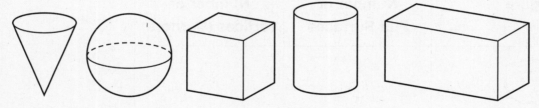

Reasoning

4. Mark the solid figure that answers the question.

I have 1 flat surface. I have 1 vertex.
Which solid figure am I?